Bass Fishing

And

Fly Fishing

A Beginner's Guide to the Necessary Skills and Techniques for Bass and Fly Fishing to Make Sure That You Use the Right Tools and Methods to Hook the Big One

By Eli Leander

Contents

Thank you for buying this book and I hope that you will find it useful. If you will want to share your thoughts on this book, you can do so by leaving a review on the Amazon page, it helps me out a lot.

Bass Fishing

for Beginners

A Beginner's Guide to the Basics and the Necessary Skills for Bass Fishing to Become an Angler Who Uses the Right Techiques and Tricks in Every Season to Hook the Big One

By Eli Leander

Foreword

What are We Fishing for Again? The Target: 'Bass' Described

Whatever the reason you had for getting these pages, you are sure to discover a quenching reprieve. Quench your thirst for knowledge and any bass fishing pursuit, challenge or battle, you will or may deal within your lifetime, right here. There is something for everybody within this book!

If your primary interest, is enhancing your capability to capture Bass, increasing, (and perhaps) even stacking the chances in your favor of being successful time and again, each time, in this angling venture and any future expedition you plan to carry out, then this book has something of value to provide you.

When you are on the hunt for Bass, understanding the fundamentals resembles the lifeline of your approach, bringing your odds alive with every cast!

ADDITIONALLY, find and establish YOUR OWN sportsman-like, angling style and character, while slowly developing your gratitude and understanding of the outdoors, as part of your fishing experience.

I provide a practical approach to the complexities and intricacies associated with this popular sport. I hope that this is captured properly by the brief title.

The focus, approach, goals and objectives are straightforward-- the basis and premise even simpler: to find out the fundamentals, get them right, regularly, with skill and mastery, and they are going to ultimately lead you to catch all the Bass you can actually desire!

I prefer to get right to the subject and aspects of our conversation-- how to discover and catch Bass! Basic yet in-depth, the text is written in such a way, that it can be put to use and work for you immediately, without spending hours reading and wading through pages of information.

The majority of published works and accomplished authors, illustrate Bass fishing as the supreme angling experience and 'The Bass' (predator- hunter itself), as tough-minded, unforeseeable, with a powerful survival instinct, fantastic awareness, sensing/sensors, that make them the keen and efficient hunters they are.

These fish gain from natures' presents of powerful sight, hearing, substantial speed, maneuverability and even jumping action moves that are going to have you catch your breath ... with wonder and exhilaration that is! All of this renders it possible for the Bass to measure up to its name and track record, as one of the "extremes" of the gaming fish populations and each angler's dream catch!

Part of the Percichthyidae family (additionally sub-classified into the genus Morone-- looked at a different unit or branch (white, yellow, striped), they are commonly distributed in temperate and tropical waters, sub-species to be discovered in fresh and saltwater. There are additionally the Australian bass (Acquaria novemaculeate), European sea bass (Dicentrarchus labrax).

Their food of choice/feed and natural diet consists of little fish, shellfishes, worms and bugs-- some anglers have actually additionally had terrific success with live-bait, like eels and even frogs.

Then there are the black bass, jointly described and including our treasured target-- called by some to be the most sporting species in The United States and Canada—the Centrarchidae family. (Largemouth and smallmouth bass, redeye, spotted, striped, black bass, Suwannee, Quadalupee).

Synthetic baits have proven helpful to the majority of anglers. Live baits are best, yet these fish can be lured, teased and drawn to strike with synthetic ones like spinners, spoons, crank-baits, surface plugs and plastic worms-- more on this a little later. Understanding what to pick (and WHY), use, switch to in particular conditions, and how to optimize this art of allure, is a crucial fundamental aspect for each striving or fantastic angler alike.

These fishes are all active predators, warming to natural baits and artificial lures. A lot of anglers would recommend spinning or trolling for freshwater fishing for Bass (bigger species) and spinning or fly-fishing for the tinier species. Saltwater aficionados may likewise take into consideration surfcasting, trolling or up-tide fishing.

Fishing for and catching Bass, in numerous waters around the world, has a proud history and custom. The majority of us are too happy to get dabbling in and form part of it, whether from boat, coast, rocks or rivers, streams, lakes or oceans. We like to tell our magnificent tales and ponder how to alter and modify, adjust and/or develop brand-new strategies, approaches to hook smallmouth, large-mouth, speckled, spotted, striped and black bass. To each of his own. You choose your favorite.

Understanding how to tell a smallmouth from a large-mouth bass, striped from spotted and so forth, is an extremely fundamental ability most anglers master rapidly. Looking particularly at the size and physical features are excellent locations to begin. Train your eye to 'find the distinctions,' so to speak.

They vary in size, markings and dorsal fins, for instance. Their upper jaws are different in length and their dorsal fins are not identical. The large-mouth has a spiny dorsal fin, highest in the center part, with practically a distinct 'break,' right before the second set of dorsal fins begin. For our buddies, the smallmouth bass, these fins are flatter, first and second are linked, with distinctive scales at the base of the second set of dorsal fins.

Apart from understanding and telling your fish species apart, by sights and/or physical qualities, there is some basic guidance I can offer right upfront. Experiencing, treading gently and honoring nature, the great outdoors, complying with the anglers' code (catch and release, licensing), environmental protection for generations of anglers (and ladies) to come, and so on are all greatly essential in your angling undertakings.

Second, preserving a general awareness, what some call "reading the waters" (comprehending the body of water, habitat to the fish, shape, depth, temperature level, stratified levels and so on), being usually, along with particularly 'observant', equipping yourself with understanding, capability and understanding of the fish, the species, the environment, and all other pertinent elements to your fishing activity and endeavors-- critical for effective process and result.

Third, (and nearly most notably), stay versatile, for change is a BIG part of this satisfying outdoor activity. It is absolutely not for the faint of heart or the impatient amongst us!

Introduction to Bass Fishing for Beginners

Understanding and Going Where the Bass Are

Bass explained: A fighter, ever-elusive, choice game-fish, predator by nature and track record, the one sought-after, valued hook, catch, reel-in and land, of many an ambitious angler.

How to catch Bass AND then catch more, bigger bass, more frequently, in more locations, with more consistency, having a proactive strategy, stacking the odds in your favor to prosper, catching more fish and taking pleasure in the process, is what this fundamental guide is all about.

The hunter ends up being the hunted-- find out how a small change in your paradigm, thinking and strategy can cause bass-angling success! Start thinking like the watery hunter, become and comprehend the bass as a hunter. Observe, know, follow, study and utilize its natural routine, preferences, patterns, practices, prey and selection of food, in your angling-strategy, and you will hav some fascinating fish- tales to tell ... And yes, we might even find out something from the ones that get/got away!

So, without further ado, let us get our rods and reels going ...

If you were told that there is one specific species of fish that the majority would refer to as tough-minded, wise, outwitting and elusively difficult to catch, then it's the Bass-- in all its shapes, sizes, versions and sub-classes.

It rings true, regardless of the context, body of water, special and/or any scenario or condition, despite tricks, pointers, proven science, strategy and all the intent in the world! Bass fishing is tough and gratifying at the same time. To guarantee hours of countless satisfaction, follow the guidelines (and add a few of your own here too!) offered here and be prepared to hook the next huge one ... consistently.

There are numerous aspects, operating in mix with the art and science, sport and pursuit that is Bass Fishing! Strategy and synergy, add to ultimate, and (I would argue), consistent and repeatable success. Tools, site, lure and ability, dawn and or dusk, shallow or deep waters, fresh/saltwater, from boat or coast-- it does not matter! There are tricks and methods for each of them.

Beginners, novices, seasonal and experienced anglers alike, are all welcome to read these pages to find some wonderful, in-demand facts about bass fishing! In the end, it is as much about the process, pleasure, understanding and admiration, as it is about the fish!

End up being a watchful, student of nature itself, the Bass' routines and patterns, whether utilizing trolling, synthetic and/or live bait, fly-fishing, on ice, fresh and salt, deep and shallow waters, do so, utilizing all to your benefit, as you undertake your own journey of the Bass!

Bass is, without a doubt, the most commonly circulated fish in North America-- often due to the convenience of our mobility and hectic society, tailored for travel and transport, Bass is within easy reach. Large-mouths, Small-mouths, striped, spotted, black bass, and so on all await.

Ever heard of a clever fish that makes measured, in-the-moment choices? One whose survival impulse is so powerful that it snatches and, at other times, absolutely disregards things and hangs around apparently withdrawn, just to strike/bite when least anticipated!

Well, that would be common of our finned, flaky (pardon the pun), fish-friend, the 'Bass.' For the purposes of this book, this species takes center-stage-- this is intentional and deliberate. Bass fishing has to do with precisely that. Tenacious, erratic and a challenge to the majority of us.

Numerous researchers have actually verified that Bass nearly 'compute' the quantity of energy it will take them to pursue the prey vs. the return. If this holds true and confirmed, what are the

ramifications for us anglers? We need to
outmaneuver them, obviously! It is all in the
fundamentals, the techniques, battle strategy,
allure, tease and strategies we select to utilize in this
process. This is going to dictate and determine our
success.

Chapter 1 - The Fundamentals of Bass Fishing

Many, if not all of the so-called 'insider' tricks, pointers and stories to tell of huge hauls of Bass, all revolve, around an extremely straightforward fundamental guideline-- comprehending the fish, (their life-cycles, feeding choices, routines and patterns and menu of choice, their nature, their relationship with the broader eco-system and position on the food-chain, timing it right.

In effect, you are setting about, producing the most favorable angling procedure and the result you can muster!

Bass fishing is a fascination, a science and an art type upon itself. It interests young and old, draws in anglers from all walks of life and both sides of the professional and amateur continuum.

One secret to bass fishing is what we can quickly refer to as, 'predictable habits.' Habits, patterns, life cycles, the natural tempo that is life and nature-- additionally relates to fish. This suggests that Bass exist within this natural actuality. If you can profit from comprehending it better, you will increase your odds of effective hooks/bites.

Looking for protective cover, foraging among rocks, stumps, weeds, sometimes on the prowl searching for prey, other times simply 'lunching' around delicately, all appear to be part of The Bass feeding routines and repertoire. Taking advantage and considering this when beginning and whenever casting is going to benefit you significantly.

Another is "competitive advantage," The Bass has an "airtight sac" (breathing bladder), that is inflatable, which allows it to swim and prosper at various levels.

A strong tail aids with speed, agility and maneuverability. It can reach considerable depths.

Other aspects like water clarity, time of day, controlled sunshine, water displacement and vibration sensing, sound level of sensitivity, all add to this fish's shrewd and making sure that you scrutinize these hints is going to increase your chances of hooking your next huge one.

Uncovering, for instance, how The Bass senses and chooses color and shade at the moment, can regularly additionally aid anglers to increase their performance. The choice and kind of lure, colors and motion, bait, and so on can all add meaningfully to your efforts.

Where the fish are ... everybody will have an answer or at least their opinion/experience on what/where/when. Nonetheless, in some cases, it is as straightforward as comprehending the habitat and those that live and prosper in it, to better engage with and delight in fishing in it-- a kind of exploring the depths, so to speak. For instance: the temperature level of the water and available oxygen determine moving patterns and disbursement of fish species. Feeding routines and preferences are distinct, falling more on the "looking alive" or live bait. Some quote smallmouth bass, as revealing an inclination for crawfish and utilizing that as an 'indication' of where these critters are going to be discovered, on the hunt for their preferred snack! Taking a look at stomach content of fish you have actually captured and kept, holds concealed hints about the food of choice-- whitefish, crawfish and others.

Having confidence, ability AND the appropriate mindset when fishing for Bass is essential. In this fight to outsmart your opponent, you will require every tool and technique available to make an effective catch. Never get dissuaded, feel beaten, or worse, give up. Bad days occur to every angler. Nature beats to its own drum, you need to find and delight in the rhythm you are so delicately part of.

Practice makes perfect-- there is no silver bullet, quick-fish technique for $9.99, that can ensure you bites and more bass constantly, anytime. It DOES take effort and dedication, determination and rigor from the angler. Some days are going to be predictably better than others. Regardless of the conditions, process and result, on a certain day put all of it down to experience and lessons learned. Log and learn, share and grow, in your own knowledge, self-confidence and toolkit, as a devoted bass angler.

Another crucial technique is, in fact, NO TECHNIQUE WHATSOEVER-- we call it an "acquired skill." It takes more of that effort we discussed before! Specific, fixed casting demands target-precision practice, enhancing your capability to put the lure precisely where you would wish it to be-- let us refer to it as 'hitting the mark.' This is another essential technique and method you can practice in the park or your living room-- attempt utilizing plugs and improve each time at regularly striking your 'target' (and absolutely nothing else we hope!).

Coming to be and being a proactive attendee in the context and environment (and process), you are in, understanding when to carry on, alter something and/or stop for the time-being (holding off the hunt or resting when needed, preparing your approach for the next trip out), is what it is all about too!

Habitual animals of comfort, The Bass (as a species), are not a lot different than a contemporary guy. Bearing this in mind is going to assist you too, as an angler. We enjoy what we enjoy, when and how we like it and typically desire it on time, when it is there and prepared, be safe, delight in life and we yearn for comfort-- food, shelter and wellness! Does this sound a lot different from our own requirements and needs? Not truly! Well, that is one way of leveling the playing field.

Comprehending the fundamental needs and niceties for these watery "animals," holds hints and advantages, for any and every angler.

Stimulus, pattern, regimen, routine-- predictors and hints-- the ace up your sleeve when absolutely nothing else works! Learn and establish abilities, to 'read' (rapidly at a glimpse, observe and make a judgment), understand intuitively what is going to occur, next and why-- find out the pattern, stay with it and exploit it to your benefit and angling success. Meet the Bass where they are, in what they do, accommodate their requirements and you are going to be shocked at what meets you in the waters beneath!

Familiarity with the Bass' favorite locations to spend time is crucial to success: Bottoms, stumps, trees, logs, weeds and plants, shapes, structures, travel-paths, creeks, shallows/deeper passages, coves, channels, bluffs, banks and coastlines-- all could be repeating hints on regular, predictable habits of the bass. The majority of the 'pros' got their understanding through reading, studying habits of their catch, in a really comparable fashion than what you are carrying out. Each time you get to know your fishy buddies a little better, up until you understand intuitively where they are going to be and where their favorite locations are. Understanding and going where the fish are becomes demystified, and much more amazing, for it is now more than an inkling or random chance-- it is an organized encounter where the watery predator ends up being the hunted!

Tools Of The Trade

Tackle, Boats, Accessories, Lures And Baits (All About Plastics, Spinners, Crank And Others- Top-Water And Specialty Lures)

Having the appropriate tools, understanding how to utilize them ideally, when and how, (additionally how not to utilize them and what they are not appropriate for) can all aid you in your bass fishing journey.

The fundamentals relating to rods, reels, line, hooks, weights, bobbers, sinkers, lures, sensors and other tools (hats, vests, nets, aromas, scissors, and so on), offer you an appreciation for having the appropriate tools for the job(s) at hand.

As an extremely participatory and stimulating sport, Bass fishing is simply nearly unrivaled in the large number of styles and tools to utilize. From peaceful streams, serene lakes to open sea and rushing rivers-- there is something for everybody.

If you are searching for fast pointers on the best tools, most fit to your purpose and the methods to master to capture bass in any conditions, may this next part enlighten and motivate you, as you dive right into the 'utilities of the fishing trade.' Several tools of the bass fishing trade we are going to be concentrating on are:

Rods, Reels, Lines and Hooks.

Tackle: Lures and Bait-- live-- artificial and, or, BUT YET ...

Restricted space does not allow big comparative descriptions or ramblings on the benefit of some tools above certain others. These debates are popular and well published in the existing literature. We take a more functional strategy and take a look at what you will, in fact, require to hook your next huge one, besides random chance and luck! I'd like to mention that selecting the appropriate tools means a great deal of different things to various individuals. Each angler has actually his/her own interpretation of what that means, varying ability level, physical qualities and strengths/weaknesses, so I will not proclaim understanding what is right for you. What I do provide are simple recommendations on which tools will stack the odds in your favor and help you indulge in preparing, rigging, baiting/hooking, recovering and landing YOUR next BIG ONE! Make sure that it does not join the droves of 'the ones that escaped'!

Even as you explore your environments and the marvel of fish species and their life cycles, patterns and habits, experimenting, hands-on with your tools and what is offered to anglers today, is part of the amazing world of Bass fishing. From fish-finders, temperature level gauges, sensors and superior technologies, to the art of preparing your lines and hooks, selecting the lures/bait most matched to your situation and function and more, contributes to the enjoyment and excitement of the activity. Preparing yourself with an understanding of these, will increase your self-confidence and practicing frequently will pay off in the long run as your know-how, exposure and fishing proficiency grows.

When it pertains to tools, the viewpoints are many and far between. Your condition, situation, purpose and objective will all figure into the last choice (oh, yes, and do not forget the ever-present budget plan and price)!

Spinning or baitcasting with artificial lures, fly-fishing, trolling with live-baits, are all choices offered to you, with professional tools on hand to help you make the most of it. Usually, a 5.5 to 7 feet rod (spinning or baitcasting), with a matching reel with 6 to ten-pound line, fast taper, single-action reel would serve you adequately. Weed-less hooks are a lifesaver in really thick cover or weeds.

Angling methods and tackle keep refining, establishing and those things nearly take on a life of its own for every single angler. There is not truly a one-size-fits-all method. This individualized relationship with your tools may imply a fundamental rod to start with, and after that, including a couple for your various expeditions and excursions-- your Bass journey has just begun. There are modern tackles and techniques, conventional or innovative, technology-driven and enabled-- whatever you fancy or prefer-- there is something for each taste and budget plan.

It is an ancient sport, pursued by many, with echoes of early hunters and anglers living off the land. Getting in touch with that timeline through hands-on activity, like bass fishing is really fulfilling. Many novices might be overwhelmed by the choice of tools available on the marketplace today. Understanding what to pick/buy, how and when to (best) apply, utilize it properly, to make the most of your odds of capturing your next huge one is crucial.

Good quality tackle is necessary-- it needs to be sufficient for whatever nature tosses your way. You are going to want to develop your toolbox of knowledge and tools in time, to react best to a few of the obstacles at hand. Excellent suitable baits and lures and how to utilize them successfully, in mix, in fast succession to guarantee bites, are other crucial elements, as is significance of preparing, presenting well, precise casting, hooking (sharpening the hooks and turning them up somewhat to make sure that the fish remain on your hook as you reel them in), along with recovering and landing of the fish.

An outstanding source for novices on all things tackle-related, equipment, fish species, tools and methods, is to be discovered in The Dorling

Kindersley Encyclopedia of Fishing: The complete guide to the fish, tackle and techniques of fresh and saltwater angling. My intention and objective here is not to reiterate the listed facts discovered here. Devoted and serious anglers are readers and want the knowledge that will increase their chances of success. This source I suggest for young and old! (There are additionally some other references listed at the end of this text, if you pick to pursue more facts and/or long for deeper insights into the art and science of Bass fishing).

All I am going to state is that having costly or the appropriate tools is not a guarantee that you are going to land the next huge one! In fishing, there are no actual guarantees. This is a 'contract' and activity in between you and nature. Exploring and getting you to the point where you understand the feel, function and ingrained strengths and disadvantages of your tools, is the genuine way to wisdom. For many trial and error, practice and perseverance are the roadways to follow to turn into skilled and experienced anglers.

Understanding the tool's complete potential will require time and practice. Remember, that sophistication in tools will establish in parallel to your own proficiency and skill-refinement.

Your desired style of fishing (from boat or shore, shallow or deep) is going to determine the most suitable option for tackle (reel and rod, line-- density and weight), line, hooks, baits and lures, weights, sinkers, leaders and more.

Whether you are a salt-water fanatic that delights in coast, beach, boat or big-game fishing or a freshwater expert favoring lure, bait, pole and/or fly fishing, there are rods, reels, lines, hooks, leaders, links, baits, and landing tackles perfect for you.

Fundamental angling methods are fairly simple to master, yet conquering and fine-tuning all the subtleties and complex moves and maneuvers, looking into the tricks (found or yet to be uncovered), of bass fishing (which has a lot of versions and settings), is going to take a lifetime of enjoyment and defeat!

Practice and take pleasure in bass fishing, according to your own niche and style, preference and place of choice-- in a word - YOUR 'specialty'. It is a really individualized and personalized pursuit and enthusiasm. Constantly keep in mind, that there is a broad selection of variety and enjoyment available, by various types of fishing places, baits and lures, and so on, to keep angling intriguing and a growing sport. It is infectious and prevalent. As soon as you are in, it is tough to let go! You are hooked and being drawn in by this sport and pastime before you know it.

For many anglers, method (and choice of tools) is determined by the species looked for, established practice, conditions and more. Mainly artificial lures are recommended and accepted for freshwater predatory fishing. Some choose live bait; others have success with tough baits such as artificial rats and plastic worms are another favorite.

Whether you are fishing from the banks, boat or float tube, the majority of people would recommend that you utilize a 6 to 6 and a half foot (1.8 -2 m) medium, heavy-push-button, spinning or bait-casting rod and reel mix, with powerful line (10-

pound). If you are fishing in weeds, heavy cover, thick, slop, grassy wetlands, swamps, and so on, a heavier line (braided) is going to serve you better/best. Hook sizes usually suggested are around a # 4 live-bait hook, honed and turned up somewhat (say around 10%). This is done to guarantee that the fish remained "hooked" and provides you a 'fighting' chance to reel it in and land it effectively. A weed-less, # 5 hook can additionally serve you well in these conditions. Large-mouth bass can be captured at any depth, utilizing live baits throughout the majority of the year (even ice fishing)! Sharp hooks are the trick.

Weights and sinkers are another aspect you need to think about, particularly in dark, cloudy waters and/or when fishing in deep water particularly. There are additionally specialized sinkers, with rattles nowadays to attract the fish much more. They are really sensitive to noises, sound and vibrations in the water-- so anything you can do to produce that appeal, tease and the temptation is fantastic to remember. Do whatever you can to activate their feeding response and guarantee a strike/bite!

Additionally, keep in mind, fish are a lot like us-- on hot, humid days, they search for shelter, food and convenience. These are their feeding grounds (no different than us, wishing to sit under an umbrella, or in front of the TV, in an air-conditioned environment, attempting to remain cool and enjoy our snack-foods!).

Understanding and thinking about these habits will assist you in capturing more fish. Search for the lily pads providing shade from the sun. Discover the ideal depth, structure and hide-away (they typically search for cover, like any other predator).

Weedy, shallow bays, hard-bottom flats, rocks, trees and/or other structures, creeks, channels, deeper waters, drops, bluffs and more can all be part of their moving patterns and habitat where they try to find food. They additionally like being close to the access point to deeper water. More later on their favored areas and how to maximize these patterns.

Instances of luring methods and how the appropriate tools can assist you:

Surface, Top-water and/or Buzz baits: Acting nearly like a spinnerbait, yet with a flat blade that allows it to surface with speed, this is a popular selection for lots of bass aficionados. It draws in the attention of the bass, by producing a disruption along the surface like a minnow, activating their basic feeding impulses and hunter impulse to strike. Rewarding you with an impressive catch!

Carolina Rig: this can quickly be referred to as just a variation of the standard, so-called 'Texas Rig' (see beneath), terrific for utilization with plastic worms or other soft bait. The majority of professional bass anglers recommend utilizing a heavier weight like 1/2 -1 oz or more. Slide the weight onto the line, follow with 3 plastic beads, a barrel swivel, and a leader line (rather tinier than the mainline). What this enables the bass angler to do is to get the bait to 'fall' to the floor with speed and is particularly suggested for fishing deep waters. The motion of the leader enables the bait to swim and rise above the bottom, and fall gradually down. For the majority of novices, this is easy to do and practice and is really flexible to get your regular rigging and tackle abilities to improve.

Crankbait: mainly describes lures, which are generally made from a range of materials, featuring tough plastic or wood. With an added feature of a diving lip on the front (simulating the motions of natural prey, wobbling, diving and swimming actions successfully), lures the bass to strike. The general rule, generally is that the bigger the lip, the deeper it can dive. Enhancements such as rattles are additionally helpful for particular conditions.

Jerk baits: An experienced favorite among bass anglers, for top-water, along with suspended bass fishing. Longer minnow-shaped plugs, available in a great deal of various sizes and colors. As a surface, top-water bait with a minor twitch-and-stop kind of retrieve, or perhaps as a more slow-and-steady retrieves underwater. Another choice is to utilize suspending jerk baits that generally dive deeper, jerking it, nearly teasing and luring the bass to come up and bite right at it.

Jigs: Some have illustrated these trusted tackle as 'lead head and hook with dressing.' Their 'included' features might take the form of rubber or plastic skirts, soft plastic baits for bodies, rather than skirts. The majority of bass specialists integrate them with a frog or plastic bait as a "follower' (plastic worm, crawfish).

Lipless Crankbait: mainly describing sinking-type lures, made from plastic, in some cases with numerous rattles inside for noise, vibrations and causing disruptions underwater.

Poppers: Topwater lures that carry a long-range punch. Retrieve with these types of lures are quick, jerky or move in one area for the duration of time. It can be rather helpful if you are attempting to find out 'where the fish are.'

Soft Jerk bait: these could be utilized for an excellent impact in the same manner as a routine jerk bait, yet can be dropped to the bottom rather effectively too to tease out our deep-water predator, swimming around for food and feast.

Spinnerbaits: an additional simulator of motion and prey on the go. It is really comparable to a jig, yet with a blade that runs above the hook, and spins to mimic a bass favorite too: fish.

Texas Rig: this is considered and called particularly for basic rigging with a plastic worm. Utilize a sliding weight, typically bullet-shaped, and a hook adequate for the size worm you have selected. Hone the hook and stick the point of the hook straight into the worm head, bring it out the side about 1/8 - 3/16" beneath the entry, thread it once more. Turn the hook around, so the point is encountering the worm's body. Lay it over the side to see where it ought to enter in order to hang directly. Position the work directly onto the hook if it is hanging. KEEP IN MIND: if the worm is twisted, your line and action are going to pay the price and it is going to be less useful.

Walking- the-dog: this is an angling method that typically needs some time to master, however, novices should not avoid trying it, for it is rather effective with bass. Casting over a reasonably long distance, enable the bait to sit for a short time period, take up the slack, and with your rod tip pointed at the water, give it a jerk to the side, then instantly move it backwards and draw in any slack, then jerk once again, and repeat all the way back.

You are, in effect mimicking the prey's evasive movements, tempting the hunter to follow, stalk and strike! This may be your ace up your sleeve for hooking YOUR NEXT BIG ONE.

Slip-bobbers, rigged with a 1/4 ounce plastic jig, live bait like a minnow, nightcrawler or leech at its tip and naturally, all on a sharpened hook.

Jiggling, gently shaking, presenting this near any emerging weeds or brush, underwater logs, trees, stumps or cover, might prove effective.

Bear in mind that fish are continuously on the move while feeding. The timing of day, amount of sunshine, the temperature level of the water, and more all factor into the angling formula.

Bobber-rigs or jigs are popular and rather effective too. Slip-sinkers, Carolina (drop-shot rig) work effectively too.

Free-line fishing in shallow waters might yield many a bass angler quite the haul. Casting a plain hook with live bait and feed the line to the bait, enabling it to 'swim' normally will draw in some certain attention.

Other professionals would suggest if you are in the so-called watery salad, weeds or heavy slop, to go heavier. 20 lb line the minimum and heavy-action, durable bait-casting rod and reel combinations with lengthy, straight handles to offer you with leverage to reel your BIG ONES in!

Drifting jig-heads, with a slip sinker rig, with 2-3 foot leader have shown to be valuable too, particularly when kept close to the bottom, watching not to get snagged while doing so. Weed-less hooks can aid you in recovering live-bait and/or that hooked fish through extremely thick underbrush.

Once again, comprehending what bass, in fact, eat, where and when, will assist you with picking and presenting the most useful, suitable and appealing bait (whether live or synthetic). Making use of the natural diet of the fish, can help you in improving your baits and lures look, technique, tactics and ultimate success.

Bass, as a predator, is going to be trying to find specific shapes, colors and familiar movements. Plastic worms and crawfish are popular options. Part of the reason bass is such a prominent species to be fishing for, is they are infamous for striking hard, biting strong and pulling strong -- a strong game fish for sure.

Spinners or spoons are synthetic baits that are particularly created for the purpose of enticing the fish. It is meant to provoke, make a strike alluring, calling on the fish's natural impulse to feed and/or protect. It optimizes your odds of securing strikes. Rotation, color, skirts, fluttering action all work together to mimic motion and take advantage of the move.

Spoons act/move in a fishlike way in the water, trolled behind boats they are usually really effective and can additionally be cast and recovered. Plugs are made of numerous materials, created particularly to float, dive beneath the surface or sink when reeling them back or in. They mimic surface disruption and lure fish with propellers or plastic skirts that move and flutter in the water.

Synthetic lures can be used alone or in the mix with live or natural baits. The size and kind of lure are going to depend upon the species, place and design of fishing you choose or pick to pursue. (For instance trolling, spinning, and fly-fishing).

For bass fishing, especially, a couple of recommendations are to keep in mind that luring the predators from below takes competency, practice and patience. For matted weed-beds and careless pitches, you may need to tickle the surface a bit. Whenever fishing in shallow waters, lures cast out quickly and recovered gradually, shaking it along, may set off a reaction. It is all in the tease and guarantees to the fish that search for indications of motion in the water.

Having an useful set of Polaroid sunglasses are a MUST! Continue moving the bait around and have fun with the presentation-- it is an art, obtained skill that improves gradually. When casting the bait out, attempt not to startle the fish, bearing in mind that they are sensitive to sound/noise, motion and vibrations.

Plastic worms work effectively (around 10"). Being versatile, switching baits, different color, and so on, utilizing a strong Texas rig, for instance, attaching a worm near the bottom of the hook, moving it onto the shank, popping it through, with a 1/2 ounce weight may be all you require!

Having a 2nd rod established and prepared to go or fishing with a pal that can assist you in reacting rapidly (as the fish are constantly on the move) and when they are prepared to strike, you are ready for them! Others recommend utilizing braided line that is more powerful than mono (for when fishing in weedy locations), without any stretch that can lessen entanglement and maximize your odds of retrieval through thick weeds and cover.

Stiff rods that can endure the "fight" bass can normally put up are another base-requirement for bass fishing aficionados. Shielding your rods with rod wraps, to minimize dings and scrapes can additionally maximize not just its performance, but keep your angling investment in good condition! Shaking and popping along bait/lures, develops a scenario that lets the fish believe the "prey" is escaping.

Nevertheless, the appropriate tools, bait, hooks and place are insufficient! Some fundamental angling methods are needed, establishing your rod and reel, understanding the fundamentals about connecting knots for joining the line to tackle, forming loops and more.

Connecting a secure knot is the main point here, as every one of them might present a 'weak point,' which you do not want when you have the BIG ONE hooked! Some recommend before tightening up a knot, to damp it with some water and cut all edges and loose ends, to prevent snag/drag.

Tube-jigs, gulp-tubes that are scented, are other choices. The soft, natural- chewy substance fools the fish into not wishing to let go and have another chew, therefore increasing your chances of landing it securely.

Top-water baits with rattles are another all-time favorite, with slack in the line, walking-the-dog (flipping) produces an appealing presentation for the fish.

Having a spinner-bait with some red in it mimics blood or injured prey to our underwater predator, activating yet again their natural impulses and feeding reaction, increasing your chances of getting a bite, hit or strike.

Whether you find yourself in a jet-boat or flat-bottom bass boat, coast, rocks, beach, cliff, stream, river, stream, lake, reservoir, or other body of water, strong rods, hot hands, great tackle, proper preparation, the appropriate bait and presentation, precise casting, where you understand the fish may be/move/feed naturally, fishing for structure and pattern, keeping an eye on surroundings and circumstances, can all make those short-lived moments of anticipation and elation initially strike momentous!

The fights, flights, turns, flips and leaps, attacks and tough hits, battles, retrieval and landing of bass, is what keeps us returning!

Let us now turn to have a look at what other considerations, plan of attack, angling methods, tricks, blunders and specialty situations can teach us about the pleasurable art and activity that is bass fishing!

Things to Think About for Bass Fishing (Return to Contents).

Water, Weather, Timing and Other Environmental Element, Facets and Factors To Consider for Bass Fishing.

As pointed out throughout this text up until now, there are numerous elements that we frequently do rule out, and/or dismiss when we initially begin angling for bass. These would involve consideration of:

Water stratification and depths (bass are discovered at differing levels and understanding where (at which level), to fish for them is critical); shallow or deep, in some cases both.

As far as water temperatures go, throughout a yearly/seasonal cycle, waters move, turn and get re-oxygenized. As temperature levels fall, from deep beneath and throughout ice forms, floats to the surface, melts and moves down once again. Science has actually supplied us with sufficient proof that 3 distinct layers form in a body of water-- say a lake, for instance. Deeper/colder, Middle-ground/milder-- transitional layer and the top/surface/warmer waters.

Heeding these levels and differing temperature levels and oxygen-rich areas are all aspects to think about even prior to going out. Think the procedure through. Think like the fish would-- ask yourself, where would you go, in all probability, if you were confronted with the identical circumstance-- the response will primarily lead you to where the fish more than likely ARE!

A temperature gauge and depth meter can all prepare you better, as an angler, well-informed and ready, to evaluate the environment, better comprehend it, gain from it, and utilize the information you collect and have on hand, to KNOW or best judge, where the fish are going to be at!

Depth is a terrific sign of what the bass are up to and where they are going to be probably discovered. This will dictate your approach, tackle and how you perform your angling abilities to land THE NEXT BIG ONE! If you fish at the appropriate level, comprehending why the fish are there, on the move, feeding, and so on, you are going to increase your chances significantly of getting strikes and hooking your next huge catch. It may even be a trophy! The depth is related to water temperature level and the optimal comfort zone of the bass-- always ask yourself what they would choose on a day like today and after that, go fish there. Measure with temperature, depth-sensing units, GPS, and so on, to determine the 'pattern' and depth of the day.

Temperature-- optimal and changing

The majority of bass species favor a temperate climate-- their metabolism is affected, if not governed practically by the surrounding waters they find themselves in. They can additionally endure quite a vast array of temperatures; for that reason, we can fish basically throughout the year. (60- 75 degrees Fahrenheit)/ It is additionally less commonly understood that ice-fishermen hook bass at around 32-39.2 degree water temperatures, in deeper waters! When it does get cooler, they get rather more sluggish, as their environment cools off substantially, and bearing this in mind is going to yield and enhance your catch.

Oxygen is additionally really crucial to fish. The hotter it gets, the closer they are going to remain to coast and to plant-life, which produces oxygen and/or where they may catch the occasional breeze. Reading these signals nature offers right, is going to prepare any angler better to go where the fish are and hook your next BIG ONE. Additionally search for areas that are not too stagnant and filled with rotting plants, as this may be an oxygen-deprived location with not a big concentration of fish-- they need to 'breathe' to survive too!

Water conditions: Clarity

Clear and/or dirty-- you are going to discover bass in both! Their behavior and mode of attack are going to alter as they plan how to ideally expend their energies in the hunt for food, survival, and so on. Predators by design, prefer cover and structure and deeper waters. When spawning, or on really hot days, you will more than likely, discover them more in the shallows.

Bass constantly have a 'back-door' access to deeper waters. These truths ought to be able to point you in the basic vicinity of where the fish are rather aptly. The male bass is additionally extremely protective of the nest/spawn site and is going to protect it, strike at any identified danger or trespasser. Fishing is no more left up to random, reflective, ruminative trial and error casting.

Now, today, substituted with more a more driven, focused, thought-through, justified and analytical competitive approach, that attempts to comprehend habits, patterns, environment, conditions, season and so on sometimes depending on the help of technology and tools to help and better your odds of identifying, finding, hooking, recovering and landing the fish effectively (primarily in deeper waters!). For that reason, if the waters are clear, head for deeper waters as a basic guideline.

Noise/Disturbances/Vibrations

DO NOT DISTURB signs are tough to place in the water! Constantly keep in mind that there is some truth to not chasing the fish away and being rather cautious and peaceful around them. The bass specifically utilizes its entire body as a sounding board. Any surface disruption, water movement and/or displacement is going to attract their attention-- this can actually aid and/or harm your angling hopes and dream.

Rusty, squeaky oars, loud motors and even the noise of a quick, far cast might interfere and/or get their attention. Understanding any, motion, identifying fish in their environment, things (water, plants) moving around, can be great indications. Wearing a great pair of Polaroid sunglasses might additionally assist you 'see' better in the intense sunshine and glare, reflections off the surface of the water(s).

Color, Sunlight, Time of day

A lot of bass anglers propose dawn and duck to be the best feeding time for the bass-- not the height of day or when the sun is at its brightest and the water might be a degree or more too warm for our fishy buddies and when they head for the deep and/or cover. It is a matter of enticing their natural impulses.

They are eager observers and motion and color have actually been examined in the bass species. Choosing a lure that resembles their prey will optimize your odds of capturing more bass. This does not indicate that they will not strike during the night, for instance, or at other times throughout the day-- you may simply need to adjust and utilize some expert methods to draw them out of hiding a bit!

Time of year: Seasons and things are a-changing!

Surroundings, weather condition and angling guidelines change and keep changing. The stage and players do not stay the exact same and even on the exact same day, daily, things will differ. This variety (the spice of life most say) is what keeps the majority of us thinking, adjusting, changing approach, bait, depth, and so on all in the continued hope and pursuit of capturing the NEXT BIG ONE.

Regarding the best time to capture bass-- viewpoints differ significantly on this subject. In some locations, fishing is just enabled after spawning. Spring, summer and fall (with fall being the very best for a lot of larger fish) and even winter some kind of bass fishing is available to you, depending upon where you are, what the weather conditions are like and what kind of year the bass are having (spawning success, health of the body of water they live and flourish in, the eco-system, stocking, pollution and so on). Even ice fishing is possible.

As mentioned previously, weather impacts habits and the season and kind of water may all require various methods, tools and bait and lures/preparation AND presentation.

As an angler, devoted bass angler, this will not faze you whatsoever! On the contrary, it supplies you with the opportunity to move gears, change approach, tools, fine-tune abilities, and discover more about your opponent and its practices. By being alert, mindful and watchful, you are going to discover a lot about the fish-- it is no longer a passive sport! Windy, low and/or high air pressure, water temperature level, choppy waves and/or surface motion of the water, cloudy skies, with a great deal of cloud cover, masking the sun, might determine whether fish are going to be biting or not. Color of plastic worms might be changed from blue (on bright days) to black (on cloudy days with not a great deal of sun around). Customizing your fishing methods and adjusting to weather patterns, even adjusting your bait/lures, approach, all bear witness of an alert bass master!

Bass are additionally sensitive to really bright sunshine, so then you may discover them searching for some shady cover and/or cooler waters. That understanding is going to prepare you well for where to go and search for them — increasing your chances of discovering them too!

Predatory Nature and creatures of habit-- what the fish themselves tell us (or not!).

Their predators of the deep are abundant in their life cycles, behaviors and patterns. It is their nature besides. They are rather predictable. As hunters, they do particular things, intuitively, and as anglers, we take advantage of it. There are great deals of truths about the types, worth understanding. Thinking like a hunter ourselves and sometimes like the fish, can boost your chances and success considerably. Being one with nature and its intricate patterns, habits, balance and quirkiness, enable anglers to be competent, accurate, well prepared and more effective, instead of leaving it up to probability and random chance to secure a bite!

Preferred habitat and fishing structures.

One author likens contour and topographic maps to bass fishermen, like treasure maps to pirates once were. Lines reveal elevation, depth, and so on. Get an idea of what the 'flooring' or bottom of the body of water (like a lake for example) would appear like-- it is hardly ever flat, typically characterized by increases and humps, slopes and drop-offs.

Slopes and access-points into deeper water ought to additionally yield more regular, bigger hauls and more strikes, as bass choose to have access to deeper waters and are continuously on the move, searching and feeding and/or protecting territory.

Natural Diet and Menu-- the art of luring fish: producing the appropriate atmosphere/conditions/allure for a strike.

Lots of things have already been said about this subject.

Confidence

The belief in your capability to find and capture the numerous bass species is, without a doubt, the very best tool of the trade to cultivate and develop in time. This can not be bought and is the personal call to every angler, to feature in his/her tackle-box!

Whether you select to utilize spinners, or swear by plastic worms, crawfish and other live bait, chum or have a preferred lure for reasons and/or tricks that are your very own, you utilize what works ideally and what you think will produce the bass you desire, want and need to have! A positive mindset goes a long way when finding out how to fish for bass. By benefiting from continuous experience, success and failure, your angling and chances are going to keep improving. Practice, in this case, is going to go a long way to allow for success in this unforeseeable, differing scenario-- when you are individually with the most popular game and sporting fish of them all: The Bass itself!

Methods For Bass Fishing Like A Pro

The Art of Precise Casting

Mastering fundamental casting is crucial. A lot of spinning and bait-casting reel and rod mixes today, are produced for hassle-free, ease-of-use versatility by a range of anglers (multi-level at that too!).

Make an effort to get rid of errors from your basic style and method. Capability and precision ought to matter more than strength and it is not constantly about getting it as far out, as quick as you potentially can (although this might be essential in particular scenarios and situations too!).

Casting, getting your line/hook/bait, sinkers, weights and leaders in and into the water, at the precise right depth, mimicking 'prey', and doing so with severe, pinpoint precision, is what this is all about. Striking your target with self-confidence is a really fundamental ability to master and fine-tune. Getting the hook out to precisely where you desired it to be is what you need to practice and work for.

Casting is one part of this procedure, getting the lure to the appropriate depth quite another. Advanced bass anglers recommend utilizing a countdown OR counting technique. Rather easy actually. From the second the bait strikes the water, begin counting, 1000, 1000 and 1, 1000 and 2, 1000 and 3 ... approximating the seconds it is going to take for it to 'drop' into the water. This is going to assist you in understanding much better what you are doing. When it strikes the bottom, for instance. Whether it got caught on something while doing so and so on. You develop reference points for yourself on and in the water.

Hands-on and rod in-hand is the very best way. Practice-plugs in the park, or your own backyard is going to make you that more successful and precise, in and on the water, no matter what the body of water, or style of fishing you pick to pursue. Whether spinning, baitcasting or fly-rodding, there is something for each taste. Even missed targets, tries and failures, are likewise great teachers, as this method is something of a routine you can master and understand.

Casting a lure with a spinning reel, casting float and/or leger rig and baitcasting are extremely similar. Lure fishing, spinning, floating, spoons, plugs, surface or top-water lures, crankbait, trolling, and so on are all standard methods that need exposure, fast demonstrations and hands-on practice. I recommend a video or DVD, or thorough online explanation, seeing a fishing program or two and getting guidelines from other anglers and specialists, in addition to finding and specifying your own style that you are comfortable and prosperous with. The appeal of bass fishing is that it provides something for everybody, no matter what your previous experience with fishing might be!

Concentrating on your grip, spinning reels, bait-casters and/or closed-face spin casters approaches and mastery, selecting a target, striving to land your lure (terminal tackle) in the middle of that target, is an excellent approach.

As a basic guideline, a great arch in the air as a travel path en route to the water is a great reference and goals to have, as you set out to enhance your casting method and precision. Line-control is essential to avoid overshooting, get a gentler landing, sluggish flight (by touching the lip of the spool with the tip of your forefinger (additionally known to anglers as 'feathering') is useful.

Playing and Landing Fish

Getting to know the feel of a fish on your hook, line and rod is extremely essential. Retrieval has to do with more than just getting the fish into the eager hands/net/boat. Proficiency, maneuvering, responsiveness, understanding of your tackle, well-balanced control, reel-clutching, fighting curves and arching/bending rods and the different controls and settings, methods (consisting of casting, hooking, playing, reeling in, recovering and landing is necessary. They are a lot more than simple steps in a process and/or sum-total of parts.

To interpret it as a real blue-blood bass-fishing experience and success, appreciation of the symphony of the interaction of procedure and result, tactics, methods, angler, tools, the catch and haul is what is at play here. When utilizing a spinning reel/bait-casting, there are 3 crucial methods to master that would include reel control:

with anti-reverse on, back winding (anti-reverse off) and thumb-pressure control.

There is absolutely nothing more amazing than a fish on the run. Apply pressure, keep the rod up a little and increase the 'drag' if needed, utilizing one of the methods above. Watch tension and stay away from line-breaks and let the fish tire.

It is one thing to prepare, cast, tease and lure, hook and ultimately reel in. The procedure, nevertheless, does not stop there. More of the mastery of standard methods consists of techniques of landing fish, like beaching (not appropriate for catch and release), tailing (not fit for all species), lipping (see the teethed species here!), netting or perhaps gaffing (prohibited in a lot of locations, due to the danger of the strike hurting the fish).

The most helpful suggestion I can offer or recommend is staying in control, not to upset or surprise the fish additionally. Enable the exhausted fish to turn, submerge the net and avoid lunging at it.

When lipping, grip the lower lip carefully between your thumb and forefingers, unhook thoroughly or keep in the water while releasing it carefully, yet effectively, without injuring the fish, sticking as far as possible, to present and approved, and catch-and-release practices.

Lure-fishing and Spinning

Spinning tackle and synthetic baits and lures are increasing in popularity and the most well-known type of fishing worldwide. As far as bass fishing is concerned, one of the simplest ways to draw in the species-- even for newbies and beginner anglers of all ages and fishing style and skill-levels. Rotation, color and motion, remaining as true as you can to the natural diet and target prey of the bass is going to maximize your odds. The shape and density of the spinning 'blade' on the lure impacts the action and mobility of the lure-- how it reacts and acts in and under water.

Floating lures are additionally popular and helpful specifically for deep-water bass fishing. Look for snagging on the bottom and make sure to weigh it done properly utilizing appropriate weights. This approach guarantees getting the bait at the eye-level of the fish.

For spoons, there are 2 broad classifications, specifically trolling and casting spoons. Weed-less lures primarily have hooks with nylon or metal weed-guards that prevent snagging and/or non-weedless spoons are additionally frequently utilized. How to tell which one to utilize, a lot of bass anglers try to find shape, weight and speed. The best way to find your way around in any tackle store or box is to practice and learn more about the habits and/or success in various conditions. Attempt to learn more about the optimal retrieval and success rates, perhaps even logging it in a personal journal as you undertake your bass journey/hunt.

Plugs, surface lures, beneficial at all fishing levels, at all speeds make these lures flexible, nimble and an all-time favorite of many a bass angler. Match the lure to the conditions you deal with and the situation, body of water and particular species you are fishing for (small-mouth, large-mouth, striped, spotted, rock, yellow, black, white, and so on). Shallow-diving crank-bait and/or surface or top-water lures have actually proven themselves most helpful for bass fishing-- excellent for fishing shallows. Stick-baits and jerking, minnow plugs (or the real thing!), prop-baits, surface disturbers, crawler-type top-water baits and even a floating, driving crank-bait can prove beneficial.

The true trick lies in what some refer to as the 'one-two punch'-- teasing and luring with a top-water or teaser (surface disturber), and after that, following it up with a plastic worm, for instance, on a 2nd rod, for maximizing strikes and yet again tipping the scales in your favor.

Plastic Worms

There are a vast array of worms offered on the marketplace (both live bait and synthetic). For passionate bass anglers, they are a requirement. The method to master is hooking them correctly. When hooking a worm for bass fishing, it is of utmost importance to make sure that you thread it effectively. Get a great deal of the body onto the hook, hooking it two times, at top and bottom. This is to make sure that it does not fly loose when you are casting it out into the water. It additionally shields it to some degree in the submerged paradise that the bass shares with other fish, who may wish to come and take a bite or sample! Utilizing worms in mix with other baits/lures and luring techniques like top-water and/or hard-bait surface disturbers or frogs, eels or whatever species and body of water would consider suitable "feeding prey" for the bass of your selection and preference is the secret. Again adjusting your approach when needed and offering the bass a range of foods to pick from, will all ideally increase your chances of hooking your next bass! ... Even if it is not yet the BIG ONE!

Chapter 2 - Mistakes and Tricks Related to Bass Fishing

As we have actually uncovered throughout these pages, there is a lot more to the bass fishing than meets the eye. As soon as you are familiar with the species, various bodies of water, various and advanced fishing and angling tools and add-ons, along with acquainting yourself with routines, patterns and nature, habits, natural diet and favored foods, mastering some fundamental abilities like preparation, presentation, tackle, bait and lures, casting precision, knots, hooks and the complexities and intricacies in retrieval and landing, the journey has began. There is a lot more to explore and discover through the adventure, sport, art and competitive science that is bass fishing.

Although, there are some last thoughts I can provide on a few of the more common casting missteps. All these 'mistakes' are well-documented in the existing literature and might quickly be overcome to maximize your bass fishing experience and haul. Here are but a couple of problems most novices struggle with:

(i) Overshot lure with excessive power in the preliminary cast and the line release not slowed

(ii) The lure falling short or being too light, with the line being released prematurely throughout the cast and/or the rod held too high after the line was released.

(iii) Lure landing too hard, because of the release at too low of an angle and not arching enough in the air.

(iv) Incorrect casting (the most frequent)-- missing the mark, where the lure goes off-course with excessive side-to-side action/motioning of the rod while casting. Practicing reel and line command, along with the overhead cast may assist.

Great deal of texts (like the Dorling Encyclopedia pointed out previously, pg. 212-213), suggests thinking of 'casting', compared to the motion of the arms on a clock- face, starting in the two o'clock position, pushing back to around the noon- position and back to the 2 again, with the rod somewhat lowered as the lure drops deeper into the water. For the majority of novices, this 'visualization' typically aids to fine-tune technique.

Chapter 3 - Styles and Specialty Bass Fishing Methods

Skipping

This method may remind you a lot of tossing rocks onto the surface of the water to see it 'skip.' As a water/top-water disruption and motion simulator, it sets off and teases our predator to come up and see what is there to eat/attack.

Spinning rods and reel combo are best utilized for this method-- ideal for fishing and reaching bass where they swim and conceal under piers, docks and pontoons. Additionally helpful for getting under and into underbrush and growth. Remember their 'comfort zone.' On bright days, bass search for shade, food and shelter and frequently rest here in shady places, under cover of structure.

Ripping

Some call this the throw it out, twitch, jerk and go technique. A medium-action rod with parabolic bend and action to it. It may, in fact, deceive our bass-friend into believing there is an 'injured' prey around. Like a professional, let the worm drop and settle to the bottom, staying there for a period of time. Reel some slack out of the line, grabbing the worm with a long, sharp upsweep of the rod tip. Let 'er rip! Let it drop down once again to the bottom, under tension while gradually bringing down the rod tip-- continue mimicking live prey like this, moving, swimming and bobbing about and your predator is going to strike it with a vengeance.

Drift Trolling

Trailing behind the boat, covering the bottom worms crawl and move, mimicking prey in its purest form. Raise and lower it sometimes, looking natural and appealing to any bass in the vicinity hunting for a yummy morsel.

Fly-Rodding

In ponds, rivers, streams and lakes this method is rather helpful. Fly-fishing methods are extremely helpful with bass. Begin by preparing and rigging a plastic worm, weed-less adding a little split-shot just before the hook. This is going to allow it to sink gradually. Flip or cast and enable it to drop and bob to the bottom. Quite the tease for the bass with eager sight, hearing and smell to miss out on. Keep the tip of the rod really low, to render it possible for you to make a timely strike when you feel a bass hit.

Night and Ice-fishing

Schooling, successful tackle and dropping the lure/bait right before the fish, not having them use up a great deal of energy is the secret for these timings and conditions. Water tends to be cooler and all your methods, techniques and strategies need to slow down a notch. Bass additionally tend to school, throughout these times. Understanding this truth can assist you in getting your target better and boosting your chances of getting a hit under these uncommon or specialized conditions.

It is practically an impossibility here to deal with each distinct condition and we hardly scratched the surface on the majority of the contexts bass anglers may find themselves. I eagerly anticipate sharing more tricks with you and learning from your journey!

Conclusion of Bass Fishing for Beginners

Catch-and-Release Fishing

Doing your part to keep nature safe and save it for future generations, is compulsory and regulated. Utilizing barbless hooks and/or extracting them quickly. Holding the fish in the water carefully while unhooking, lessening the trauma and damage to the fish is vital. Support the fish and let it go with the present, swimming away and left to live another day, for numerous fights more to come!

Do all you can to comprehend and stick to licensing, permits, closed season terms, minimum size and catch restrictions. These and other measures exist to protect and serve, to lessen the threat of over-fishing and species ending up being extinct.

This may not be the finest book on bass fishing ever written, yet might the passion and contents motivate you to success as a devoted and effective angler. If I can fire up self-confidence and hints of exhilaration for fisher-folk, young and old, then these pages have actually done well!

May the road (and the waters, The Bass), come up to meet you. May your journey and journal grow, with each entry teaching more, increasing self-confidence and ability!

May the delights of Bass fishing and the many ways we can select actively to partake in it, bring you continued and continuous pleasure, reward, haul and tremendous enjoyment!

Appendix

Action - Measure of rod effectiveness that illustrates the elapsed time between flexion and return to straight setup; ranges from slow to quick, with slow being the most amount of flexion; additionally describes the durability of the rod (light, medium and heavy) with light being a limber rod and heavy a stout rod; additionally describes gear of reels.

Active Fish - Bass that are feeding greatly and striking boldy.

Adaptation - Biological modification that boosts fitness.

Algae - Simple plant organisms.

Alkalinity - Measure of the quantity of acid-neutralizing bases.

Alley - An opening between spots of emerging weeds; additionally the parallel area separating emerging weeds and the coastline.

Amp - Measure of electrical current.

Amp Hour - Storage capability measurement of a deep-cycle battery acquired by multiplying the current circulation in amps by the hours that it is created.

Angler - Individual utilizing pole or rod and reel to capture fish.

Anti-reverse - System that stops reels from spinning in reverse.

Backlash - Tangle of line on a bait-casting reel because of spool overrun.

Backwater - Shallow area off a river.

Bag Limit - Limitation on the amount of fish that an angler might acquire in a day.

Bail - Metal, semicircular arm on an open-face spinning reel that engages the line after a cast.

Bait - A synthetic lure is generally what is implied despite the fact that bait can additionally indicate live bait.

Baitcasting - Fishing with a revolving-spool reel and baitcasting rod; reel installed on the topside of the rod.

Baitfish - Little fish frequently consumed by predators.

Bar - Long ridge in a body of water.

Basic Requirements - Describes the 3 survival requirements of bass: reproduction, safety, and food.

Bay - Significant imprint on the coastline of a lake or reservoir.

Bite - When a fish takes or touches (or hammers) a bait to ensure that the angler feels it. Additionally called a hit, bump, or a strike.

Black Bass - Typical term utilized to explain numerous kinds of bass, including the largemouth, smallmouth, and spotted bass.

Blank - Fishing pole without grip, guides or finish.

Brackish - Water of intermediary salinity between seawater and freshwater.

Break - Distinct variation in otherwise continuous stretches of cover, structure, or bottom type. Generally anything, that "separates" the underwater terrain.

Break line - A line of abrupt change in depth, bottom type, or water clearness in the feature of typically consistent structure. A location where there is an unexpected or extreme change in the depth of the water, or weed type. This might be the edge of a creek, a submerged cliff, or perhaps a stand of submerged weeds.

Brush line - The interior or the outside edge of a stretch of brush.

Brush pile - Typically describes a mass of little- to medium-sized tree limbs lying in the water. Brush piles might be only one or two feet across, or they might be very big and they might be noticeable or submerged. They can be produced by Nature or manmade. They typically hold fish. And anglers.

Bumping - Describes the act of making a lure hit a thing such as a log, tree, or pier piling in a measured manner. This is frequently done inadvertently but can get the identical response from the fish.

Buzzbait - Topwater bait with big, propeller-type blades that churn the water throughout the retrieve.

Made up of a leadhead, stiff hook, and wire that supports several blades.

Buzzing - Recovering a lure, like a spinnerbait or buzzbait, at a rate quick enough to trigger it to stay partly out of the water, triggering a loud disruption. Often called ripping or burning.

Cabbage - Any of numerous types of weeds, situated above the surface or underwater, of the genus Potamogeton.

Carolina Rig - A style of terminal tackle typically utilized to keep a lure a foot or two (or more) off the bottom. This is most typically utilized with a plastic worm, yet is additionally utilized with floating crankbaits and other lures too. A barrel slip sinker of 1/2- to 1-ounce is first slipped on the line, and after that, a swivel is connected to the end of the line. A bit of line 18 to 30 inches long is then connected to the other end of the swivel, and a hook or lure is connected to the end of this piece line. Rigged Texas-style (weedless with the hook buried in the body of the bait), the mix is outstanding for fishing ledges, points, sandbars, and humps.

Channel - The bed of a stream or river.

Chugger - Topwater plug with a dished-out (concave or "cupped") head created to make a splash when pulled forcefully.

Clarity - Describes the depth at which you are able to observe an item (such as your lure) under the water.

Cold Front - A weather condition accompanied by high, clear skies, and an unexpected decrease in temperature level.

Contact Point - The deepest position on a structure where a bass angler can initially successfully present his lure to bass as they move from deep water.

Controlled Drift - The act of utilizing an electrical motor, drift sock, or oars to let drift to be achieved at a specific speed and/or direction. This term is typically called "drift fishing" by many anglers.

Coontail - Submerged aquatic plant of the hornwort family usually discovered in hard water; identified by stiff, forked leaves.

Cosmic Clock - The sun's seasonal impact on water and weather relating to barometric pressure, wind, and cloud cover.

Count It Down - Timing a sinking lure to identify when it is going to reach a defined depth. This is achieved by discovering the rate of sinking of a lure in feet-per-second. Frequently utilized when fishing for suspended fish.

Cove - An imprint along a shoreline.

Cover - Natural or manmade things on the bottom of lakes, rivers, or impoundments, specifically those that sway fish habits. Anything a fish can utilize to hide itself. Examples consist of stick-ups, tree lines, stumps, rocks, logs, pilings, docks, weeds, boathouses, duck blinds, bushes, and so on.

Crankbait - Normally, a lipped lure that dives under the surface throughout the retrieve. So-called lipless crankbaits are slim, minnow-like lures that sink at a rate of about 1-foot every second.

Dabbling - Working a lure up and down in the identical area a dozen or more times in a bush or next to a tree.

Depthfinder - A sonar gadget, either a flasher system or LCR recorder, utilized to read the bottom structure, identify depth, and sometimes, in fact, find the fish; additionally called a fishfinder.

Disgorger - Device for getting rid of hooks deeply ingrained in the throat of fish.

Drag - Device on fishing reels that lets the line to pay out under pressure, although the reel is engaged. When set properly, it assures versus line breakage.

Drop-Off - An abrupt boost in depth, developed by gulley washes, little creek channels, land points, and the basic lay of the land.

Drop Shot - A hook connected straight to the line from four-inches to four-feet above the sinker. The hook is connected from the rear or opposite the point, with an easy Palomar knot with a tag end about 4 or 5 feet long. The weight hangs and the hook is at a 90-degree angle to the line with the hook point up. The hook could be 18 to 24 inches above a bell sinker connected on with a slip- knot.

Ecology - The branch of biology handling the connection between organisms and their habitat.

Edge - Describes the borders developed by a change in the structure or greenery in a lake. Some instances of edges are tree lines, weed lines, and the edge of a drop-off.

Euthrophic - Extremely fertile waters distinguished by warm, shallow basins.

Fan Cast - Making a series of casts just a couple of degrees apart to encompass a half-circle

Farm Pond - Little manmade body of water.

Feeder Creek - Tributary to a stream.

Feeding Times - Particular times of the day when fish are most active. These are connected with the position of the sun and moon and are described as solunar tables (additionally called moon charts) and are predictable for any time and location. See Moon Times.

Filamentous Algae - Kind of algae identified by long chains of connected cells that provide it a stringy feel and look.

Feeding Cycle - Specific regular periods throughout which bass satisfy their cravings. Examples: Significant or Minor Solunar durations; sunrise, sundown.

Finesse Fishing - An angling method defined by the use of light tackle - line, rods, reel and synthetic baits (typically tube worms, grubs, or other small-sized soft-plastic lures); typically effective in clear, relatively uncluttered water.

Flat - A spot in a body of water with little if any change in depth. Little and big, flats are typically surrounded on at least one side by deeper water, the bottom comes up to create a flat location where fish are going to typically go up for feeding.

Flipping - (typically shortened to flippin') The method of positioning a lure in a given area specifically, and silently, with as little disruption of the water as possible utilizing an underhand cast while managing the line with your hand.

Flipping Stick - Heavy action fishing pole, 7 to 8 feet long, created for bass fishing.

Florida Rig - Extremely comparable to the Texas Rig, the only distinction is the weight is secured by "screwing" it into the bait.

Fly 'N Rind - Identical thing as jig-and-pig - a mix of a leadhead jig and pork rind trailer.

Forage - Little baitfish, crayfish and other animals that bass consume. Might additionally be utilized in the sense of the bass searching for food (foraging).

Front - Weather system that results in modifications in temperature level, cloud cover, rainfall, wind and barometric pressure.

Gear Ratio - Measure of a reels' retrieve velocity; the amount of times the spool revolves for each total turn of the handle.

Grayline - Grayline lets you compare strong and weak echoes. It "paints" gray on targets that are more powerful than a predetermined value. This enables you to tell the difference between a tough and soft bottom. For instance, a soft, muddy or weedy bottom returns a weaker symbol, which is shown with a slim or no gray line. A tough bottom returns a powerful signal, which leads to a broad gray line.

Grub - A brief plastic worm utilized with a weighted jig hook.

Habitat - The location in nature where a plant or animal species lives. The water, greenery, and all that comprises the lake, which is where bass reside. Habitat, for other animals, is additionally in the woods and cities, it's generally a term utilized to suggest a "living location" or home environment.

Hard Bottom - Location in a body of water with a strong base - clay, gravel, rock, sand. The kind of bottom where you would not sink far, if whatsoever, were you to step on it.

Hawg - Typically describes a lunker-size or heavyweight bass weighing 4 pounds or more.

Holding Location - Structure that repeatedly holds 3 to 5 catchable bass.

Holding Station - Put on a lake where non-active fish spend the majority of their time.

Honey Hole - An great fishing area consisting of a variety of huge bass; likewise, any location with a big concentration of keeper bass.

Horizontal Motion - The distance a fish moves while staying at the identical depth.

Hump - A place higher than the surrounding location. A submerged dam or island may be taken into consideration as a hump.

Ichthyology - The branch of zoology that handles fishes - their category, structure, routines, and life history.

Non-active Fish - Bass that remain in a non-feeding state of mind. Examples of usually inactive times: following a cold front; throughout a significant weather change that results in an abrupt increase or fall in water temperature, or when an increasing lake level is quickly reduced.

Inside Bend - The inside line of a grass bed or a creek channel.

Isolated Structure - A possible holding area for bass; examples consist of a single bush on a point, a midlake hump, or a big tree that has actually fallen under the water.

Jig - A leadhead put around a hook and including a skirt of rubber, plastic, or hair.

Jig-N-Pig - Mix of a leadhead jig and pork rind trailer; amongst the most helpful baits for drawing in trophy-size bass.

Keeper - A bass that complies with a particular minimum length limitation developed by tournament companies and/or state fisheries department.

Lake Modification Sources - Components that alter bodies of water, like ice action, wave action, and erosion.

Lake Zones - Classification that consists of 4 classifications: shallow water, open water, deep water, and basin.

Laydown (or Falldown) - A tree that has actually fallen into the water.

Light Strength - The quantity of light that can be gauged at specific depths of water; the higher the strength, the further down the light is going to project. This measurement can be considerably impacted by wind conditions and water clearness. In waters where light strength is low, vibrantly colored lures are wise options.

Line Guides - Rod rings through which fishing line is passed.

Lipless Crankbaits - Synthetic baits created to look like a swimming baitfish. Such plugs vibrate and/or wobble throughout retrieve; some have integrated rattles. Likewise called swimming baits.

Livewell - An oxygenated tank in boats utilized to hold fish in the water up until weigh-in time so that they have a greater possibility of survival when launched. Comparable to an aquarium.

Logjam - A group of horizontal logs pressed together by wind or water circulation to form a blockage. In lakes, logjams are normally discovered near the coast and in the backs of coves.

Loose-Action Plug - A lure with broad and slow motions from side to side.

Lunker - Usually, a bass weighing 4 pounds or more.

Micropterus Salmoides - Scientific term for largemouth bass.

Migration Route - The course followed by bass when moving from one location to another.

Milfoil - Surface-growing water plants.

Mono - Brief for monofilament fishing line.

Moon Times - 4 stages of the moon are generally what the angler is interested in. Typically, the "ideal times" in a month take place 3 days prior and 3 days after, and consist of the day of the new or full moon. First-quarter and second-quarter durations are considered as just "good times."

Off Color - Describes the color and/or quality of the water. Brown is muddy like from rain runoff, greenish from algae and black from tannic acid are the typical off-color conditions.

Our Hole - Proprietary term utilized by anglers to define the location where they intend to fish(My hole, their hole, and so on). Although, in fact, all holes are all angler's holes considering that the lakes being fished are primarily public water. It's just your hole if you arrive initially. Otherwise, it's their hole.

Outside Bend - The exterior line of a creek channel or grass bed could be considered on outside bend.

Oxbow - A U-shaped bend in a river.

Pattern - A specified set of place and presentation elements that regularly produce fish. Example: If you capture more than one fish off a pier or stick-up, then your odds of capturing more bass in such locations are exceptional. This is typically called "establishing a pattern."

Pegging - Putting a toothpick in the hole of a slip sinker to stop the sinker from moving along the line. Other products such as rubber bands slipped through the sinker have actually additionally ended up being popular and don't snag line.

PFD - Initials that stand for Personal Floatation Device; additionally referred to as a life vest.

pH - This is a measurement for liquids to figure out whether they are acidic or alkaline. On a scale of 1 to 10, 7 is taken into consideration as neutral. Beneath 7 the liquid is acidic and above 7 it is alkaline. This is an aspect that plays a role in the health of the lake and the fish in addition to where the fish might be discovered in a lake.

pH Meter - Just as a thermometer gauges cold and heat, a pH meter can be utilized to measure the level of acidity and alkalinity of water. The pH scale varies from 0 to 14. Bass usually choose water that is somewhat alkaline in the 7.5 to 7.9 range. Water with a pH less than 7 is acidic. Once prominent amongst significant bass anglers, the device is no longer commonly utilized.

Pick-Up - The action of a bass taking a gradually fished lure, like a plastic worm, crawfish or lizard.

Pit - Location excavated for mining operations that fills with water.

Pitching - Presentation method in which worms or jigs are dropped into cover at close range with an underhand pendulum movement, utilizing a 6 to 71/2 foot baitcasting rod. The act of pitching bait into a pocket or under tree limbs. Comparable to flipping, however, it demands less stealth and is generally carried out from further distances.

Pocket - A little imprint of the coastline.

Point - A finger of land jutting into the water; deeper water is normally discovered simply beyond the exposed tip and along the length of both sides. Fishing on and around points is frequently incredibly satisfying. They generally hold fish.

Post Front - The duration following a cold front; atmosphere clears and ends up being bright; generally identified by strong winds and a substantial drop in temperature level.

Presentation - A collective term describing the selection of the kind of lure, color, and size; structure targeted; the quantity of disruption a bait makes when getting in the water; and retrieval method, speed, and depth utilized to capture fish. This describes the situations and manner (speed and direction, and so on) in which a lure is demonstrated to a fish.

Pro - A very few of the country's leading bass anglers can really claim the word pro. Not only should the pro be a constant cash winner on the major tournament circuits, yet he/she should additionally be articulate, an excellent salesman, provide a clean-cut image, and have the capability to teach others to capture fish.

Professional Overrun - A respectful term for backlash.

Revolving-Spool Reel - Another term for a baitcasting reel. The spool turns throughout the casting, unlike the spindle of a spinning or spincasting reel.

Reservoir - Synthetically developed location where water is gathered and kept; additionally called an impoundment.

Riprap - A manufactured stretch of rocks or material of a difficult structure that typically extends above and beneath the coastline; typically discovered near dams of huge impoundments.

Saddle - A site where structure narrows before expanding once again.

Sanctuary - Deep-water bass habitat.

Scatter Point - Position along the structure where bass begins to separate or spread; frequently discovered in shallow water, at or really near to a breakline.

Short Strike - When a fish strikes at a lure and misses it.

Slack Line - The loose line from the tip of the rod to the lure. This could be a minor bow in the line to an excess of line resting on the water.

Slicks - Bass not long enough to fulfill tournament requirements; normally less than 14 inches. Such fish additionally are called "nubbins ", "through backs", "pop corns", "babies" and "dinks".

Slip Sinker - A lead weight with a hole through the center. Threaded on line, a slip sinker slides easily backwards and forwards.

Slough - A long, narrow stretch of water like a little stream or feeder tributary off a lake or river.

Slow Roll - Spinnerbait presentation in which the lure is recovered gradually through and over cover items.

Slush Bait - Topwater plug with a flat or pointed head.

Spincaster - A way of fishing utilizing a push-button, closed-face spinning reel and baitcasting rod; reel is installed on the topside of the rod.

Spinnerbait - A leadhead lure comparable in shape to an open safety-pin with a hook; other features consist of rubber, plastics, or hair, and a couple of blades of different sizes and shapes.

Spinning - A way of fishing using an open-face or closed-face spinning reel; reel is installed on the underside of the rod; rod guides are on the underside of the rod.

Split Shotting - Typically referred to as stitch fishing since you move the bait in increments no larger than a sewing stitch and made just as gradually and patience is the trick. Utilize a little # 5 split-shot and crimp it about 18 inches above a light wire 1/0 or lighter little hook. Spinning tackle is a necessity. Little worms, 3-inch salt craws and others are best for the mild application needed.

Spook - The act of startling a fish in an unfavorable way. Examples: too much noise, casting a human shadow.

Stick-Up - Fixed structure - stump, limb, part of a pipe, fence post - that extends about 5 feet or less above the surface; a preferred casting target of bass anglers.

Stragglers - Bass that stay near the coast following a general migration.

Stringer - Old-fashioned term for a limitation of fish, utilized by tournament anglers to show their catch (10-pound stringer = 10 pounds of fish). Not in fact utilized any longer to keep bass, simply a term individuals can't appear to stop utilizing.

Structure - Modifications in the shape of the bottom of lakes, rivers, or impoundments, particularly those that affect fish habits. This is most likely the most misconstrued word in bass fishing. Structure is a feature on the bottom of the lake. Some instances of structure are creeks, humps, depressions, sandbars, roadbeds, ledges, and drop-offs. Some instances that are not structure: a stump, tree, or brush pile.

Suspended Fish - Bass at midlevel depths, neither near the surface nor on the bottom.

Swimming Lures - Sinking-type synthetic baits created to look like a swimming baitfish. Such plugs vibrate and/or wobble throughout retrieve; some have integrated rattles. Additionally referred to as lipless crankbaits.

Tail-Spinners - Compact, lead-bodied lures with a couple of spinner blades connected to the tail, and a treble hook suspended from the body; developed to look like an injured shad; helpful on schooling bass.

Taper - A location in a body of water that slopes towards deeper depths.

Terminal Tackle - Angling tools, leaving out synthetic baits, connected to the end of a fishing line; examples consist of hooks, snaps, swivels, snap-swivels, sinkers, drifts, and plastic beads.

Texas Rig - The technique of fastening a hook to a soft-plastic bait - worm, lizard, crawfish, to ensure that the hook is weedless. A slip sinker is threaded onto the line, and after that, a hook is connected to the end of the line. The hook is then placed into the head of a worm for about one-quarter of an inch and brought through up until just the eye is still embedded in the worm. The hook is then spun and the point is ingrained somewhat into the worm without coming out the opposite side.

Thermocline - The layer of water where the temperature level changes at least half a degree per foot of depth. Generally, a layer of water where increasing warm and sinking cold water meet.

Tight-Action Plug - A lure with brief, fast side-to-side motion.

Tiptop - Line guide at top of the fishing pole.

Topwaters - Drifting tough baits that produce some degree of surface disruption throughout retrieve.

Trailer Hook - The additional hook, or cheater hook included in a single-hook lure, like a spinnerbait or weedless spoon.

Transition - The imaginary line where one kind of bottom material changes to another.

Treble Hook - Hook with single or bundled shaft and 3 points.

Triggering - Employment of any lure-retrieval method or other fishing method that induces bass to strike.

Trolling Motor - A little electrical fishing motor, usually installed on the bow, that is utilized as secondary boat propulsion, for boat positioning, and to navigate silently in fishing locations.

Turnover - The duration when the cold water on the surface of a body of water comes down and is substituted by warmer water from beneath.

Vertical Motion - Up and down motion of fish. It can additionally be a motion of a lure like a spoon (vertical jigging).

Weedless - A description of a lure created to be fished in heavy cover with a slightest amount of snagging.

Weedline - Abrupt edge of a weedbed brought on by an alteration in depth, bottom type, or other aspects.

Wormin - The action of fishing with a plastic worm, lizard, crawfish, or comparable bait.

Fly Fishing

Guide

A beginner's Guide of 100 Tips Which Will Show You the Basics of Fly Fishing so That You Pick the Right Spot, Use the Right Gear and Techniques and Avoid a Lot of Beginner's Traps

By Eli Leander

Introduction of Fly Fishing Guide

Fly fishing is an incredibly popular fishing sport that can be both unwinding and challenging simultaneously.

The following suggestions and techniques are perfect for novices. When you're simply beginning learning to fly fish, you'll want all the aid and suggestions that you can receive from the professionals.

Fly Fishing Tips

Tip # 1: Practice your Casting

The professionals state that the one thing that you need to do to establish an excellent casting method is to practice as frequently as you can. This will result in effectiveness in casting that makes all the difference between being an effective fly fisher or a disappointed one.

Attempt practicing against a wall on the outside of your home. Simply envision that there is a clock hanging on the wall that is at the same level as your shoulder. Place markers, such as black electrical tape, at the 11:00 and 1:00 clock positions. Practice casting against these markers for a couple of minutes every day to enhance your precision and style.

Tip # 2: Rods

There are a number of things that you want to think of when selecting the ideal kind of rod for you.

Every reel and rod has a particular function that you need to be familiar with.

Among the first things that you need to think about is comfort. Is the rod that you're utilizing comfy for you to hold? If you're shorter than about 5' 5" you will not wish to utilize a rod that is 7 feet. Select a rod length that is simple for you to hold and cast for a couple of hours at a time.

The majority of the rods on the marketplace today are created to permit you to feel when a fish bites. The shaft of the rod is referred to as a "blank" and when the rod is first made, the blank is made from fiberglass, graphite, or other components. Each of these blanks has an action that is either: light, medium, medium/heavy, or heavy. The upper part will likewise have an action that is either: extra light, light, or standard.

Both ends of the blank are put together and the outcome is a fishing rod, complete with a handle and guide. Regardless of what kind of rod you're utilizing, the "action" of the rod will describe the "blank." The action of the rod will have a good deal to do with the kind of fishing that you're doing.

Tip # 3: Holding your Rod Properly

It is essential that you know to hold your rod successfully under any fishing conditions. You wish to ensure that you keep excellent control at all times without grasping too hard. You can change the power of your hold when you're in the middle of a cast. This will permit you to lessen the vibrations of each motion. With simply a little bit of practice, you'll have the ability to increase the tightness while understanding how to loosen up your grip.

Tip # 4: What to Do to With a Running Fish

Be prepared if a fish runs towards you. Stand on your toes and simultaneously raise your rod up over your head as high as you can. Take the line and place it back over onto your 2nd and third fingers of the hand that is holding the rod. Rapidly strip the line to pull up on any slack.

If the fish begins to escape from you ensure that you keep the rod up high and gradually let out the line, letting it move from your fingers. Be prepared to palm the reel of the rod when the slack is totally gone.

Tip # 5: Finest Bait Options

Following is a list of some finest bait options as advised by the professionals:

- Grubs: Grubs are little lures that are generally utilized to capture bigger fish. Grubs are excellent for usage in highland reservoirs where there is little cover for the fish. The grub is similar to a bare jig head that has a soft plastic body to connect to the hook. You'll wish to utilize them frequently in clear water conditions.

- Jigs are best utilized in water that is clear to dirty and in water temperature levels that are beneath 60 degrees. The jig is thought about to be a "presentation" lure and the perfect method to utilize them is by making them look as alive as you can. The jig is basically lead-weighted bait that has one hook. You'll wish to add a trailer to the end of the hook for the greatest outcomes.

- Plastic worms: If you wish to capture that trophy fish, you'll most likely wish to utilize a plastic worm. This is due to the fact that the plastic worm is among the most reliable lures for capturing any kind of big fish. Plastic worms have a thin and long profile with a natural action that attracts them quickly to bass. You'll need to find out how to utilize a plastic worm by touch, feel, and practice. The more that you practice, the better outcomes you'll attain. Something that you want to remember is that the fish wants to see the worm before it will strike it. For that reason a plastic worm is best utilized in clear water.

- Lure color: Select lures that are all black or all white. A mix of black and red likewise works rather well. There will be an odd time when fluorescent colors, such as bright yellow or green, will work properly; however, you'll want to experiment with this.

Tip # 6: Keep your Dry Flies Floating Longer

One manner in which you can keep your dry flies floating higher and longer atop the water is by waterproofing them. Take a can of Scotch-guard, the identical things that you utilize to shield your furnishings, and spray those flies that you intend on taking fishing with you in the next couple of days. Let them dry over night prior to utilizing them.

The Scotch-guard will put a water-resistant protective coating around your flies and prevent them from ending up being soaked with water. This will permit them to float higher and longer on the water.

Tip # 7: Kinds of Reels

Reels-- There are 3 primary kinds of reels that you can pick from when it pertains to fly fishing: (1) baitcasting reels, (2) spinning reels, and (3) spincast reels. The reel that you select will depend upon your own individual preferences.

Baitcasting reels: Baitcasting reels have much better precision and control of the lure than other reels. They are much better geared up to manage lines that are 10 or more pounds in weight. Something to be knowledgeable about when utilizing a baitcasting reel is that they frequently have the propensity to snarl or resist when the spool begins to spin faster than the line that is being played out. This is especially accurate if you are casting into the wind.

To prevent these reactions, baitcasting reels have a magnetic braking function; however, you'll wish to count more on the control of the spool stress, which is a knob that is normally situated right next to the handles. You'll want to set the spool tension knob for each lure by holding the rod directly and disengaging the spool. Loosen up the tension simply up until the lure starts to fall and after that, tighten up the spool only a bit.

When you're casting the reel you'll disengage the spool, and after that, hold it tight with your thumb. When you wish the lure to move forward, you'll just loosen up on the pressure. After some practice, you'll discover how to manage the speed of the spool so that you have much better precision.

Spinning reels: Spinning reels are reels that have a spool that is fixed. The line is spun onto the spool as a gadget called a "bail" turns around it. Spinning reels can be utilized for any size of line; however, more skilled fly fishers will utilize it for light-weight lures with a weight under 10 pounds. Spinning reels tend to be a better choice than baitcasting reels when you're casting into the wind.

One drawback of using a spinning reel is that there is the inescapable twisting of the line, which is going to develop tangles and knots. When your line ends up being twisted, the very best thing that you can do is substitute the line with a brand-new one. One manner in which you can prevent a few of these tangles from happening is by putting the spool into a glass of water for about 24 hr before you head out to fish, offering it an opportunity to soak.

To cast the spinning reel, hold the handle of the rod with one hand, making certain that the spinning reel is on the bottom side with your middle finger put in front of the "foot" of the reel. Gradually open the bail and pull the line behind the initial knuckle of your forefinger. Discharge the line by pulling your forefinger into a straight position. You can manage how far you cast the line by letting the line move along your forefinger as near to the spool as possible as the line relaxes. When you wish to stop the line you merely press your finger versus the lip of the spool.

Spincast reels: Spincast reels are likewise called "push button" reels. They are closed-face and are really easy to use. They are nearly impossible to tangle and could be cast in smooth, long arcs without twisting. The primary part of the spool is enclosed in a covering and it stays in one location while a pick-up pin spins around the spool. When purchasing a spincast reel, ensure that you don't buy the most affordable one because you wish to spend on good quality. Lots of newbie fly fishers succeed with a spincast reel.

To cast the spincast reel, all you want to do is to depress the push button and hold it down. You'll discharge the button when you wish that your lure moves in a forward position.

Tip # 8: Tying Effective Knots

Very few knots are going to ever be at 100% of the ranked strength for a line. Nevertheless, if you dampen your knots before you pull them tight, they will be far more useful. Other things that you can do to connect a much better knot involve:

- Tighten them extremely gradually.

- Watch out for any weak frays.

- Test every knot by making certain to pull it hard.

These methods will minimize the possibility of a knot failure happening at that moment when you least desire it.

Tip # 9: Securing your Fly Line

There are numerous things that can harm your fly line that include: casting the line without a leader, stepping on the line, or pinching the line in between the frame of the reel and the spool. Take actions to prevent these dangers. There are likewise numerous liquid things that can harm your fly line. Make certain that you keep the line far from an insect repellent, sunblock, fuel, and some line cleaners.

Tip # 10: Cleaning your Fly Line

Keeping your fly line is necessary for the functionality of your fly fishing. Dirt will get on your line from algae that are discovered in the waters where you fish. With time the dirt will get on your line and this can trigger your line to end up being stripped down. You'll understand when your fly line is too filthy due to the fact that it will not float, nor will it move efficiently through the rod guides.

Cleaning your fly line is simple: utilize a cleaning pad that you can purchase at the majority of angling shops. Or you can likewise clean the fly line with a couple of drops of a moderate soap (stay away from detergents). Simply rub the line carefully with a wet fabric.

Tip # 11: Storing your Fly Line

Your reel is the safest location for you to have your line. The only thing that you want to make sure of is that your line isn't subjected to chemicals, high heats, direct sunshine, or solvents. There will be times when your line has actually been kept for a while and it will coil. If this happens you want to extend it gradually; it will quickly begin to give and you can utilize it securely once again.

Tip # 12: Kinds Of Fly Lines

The majority of the lines that you'll utilize for fly fishing will be made from nylon monofilament. Nevertheless, other lines are ending up being just as popular such as lines that are (1) braided, (2) co-filament, or (3) fused. Regardless of what kind of line you purchase, make certain that it's a "premium" line. Premium lines are more long-lasting and even more affordable. You'll wish to match the fishing line that you purchase to the following requirements and conditions:

- Strength: Strength is determined in pounds of force that is required to break the line. You'll discover that a lot of lines will break at greater weights than they are sold at.

- Resistance to Abrasion: When you're fishing in locations where there are a great deal of brush or rocks, you'll wish to utilize a line that will not break quickly when it is continuously rubbed.

- Line Diameter: The diameter of the line will impact the method the line is cast along with how deep your lure will run. Diameter likewise has an impact on the visibility of the line. The thinner a line is, the harder it will be for the bass to see it. Thinner lines will likewise provide some bait, such as grubs, a more reasonable flowing action. The one advantage of lines with a thicker diameter is that they are much better able to endure abrasion.

- Stretch Lines: Stretch lines will not break as quickly when they are being pulled by a fish. They are helpful in letting you spot strikes as well as aiding you with setting hooks.

- Line Stiffness: The stiffness of the line is associated with its stretch. The stiffer the line is, the more difficult it will be to cast. The benefit of having a stiff line is that it is more delicate than flexible lines.

- Line visibility: In clear water, it is necessary that your line is as unnoticeable to the fish as possible. Nevertheless, you'll wish to have a line that is extremely noticeable when your fishing lures are on a subtle strike, such as worms, grubs, and jigs. This is so that you can quickly discover any motion on the line that might suggest a fish is biting.

Tip # 13: Pinching your Hooks

Take some time to pinch the barbs on the ends of your hooks. This will prevent scratches. And remember that a hook that is barbless is simpler to remove that one that is barbed.

Tip # 14: Lures

Following is a list of lures that are typically suggested by the skilled fly fishers that you one day wish to match in ability:

- Spinnerbaits: Spinnerbaits are among the most flexible of all fly fishing baits. This is since they can be utilized at nearly any time of the year in any kind of weather or water condition. You'll likewise have the ability to utilize spinnerbaits in any kind of cover.

- Crankbaits: Lots of expert fly fishers utilize crankbaits due to the fact that they behave much as "bird dogs" when it pertains to hunting for fish. This kind of lure is terrific in deeper waters, given that it can dive deep. You'll wish to utilize a rod that is between 6.5 and 7 feet if you wish to utilize crankbait.

- Tube jigs: Tube jigs are fantastic when you're fishing in clear water where the fish are inactive. These jigs have actually been created to be utilized as drop bait. The tube jig is utilized usually in water that is 10 feet or deeper.

- Vibrating lures: Vibrating lures are made from metal or plastic. They produce a tight vibration when they are drawn back in. This kind of bait will sink quickly and is best utilized in deeper waters.

- Jigging spoons: Jigging lures are called "structure lures" and are utilized frequently by knowledgeable fly fishers. These lures work extremely well in deep water when you are fishing for suspended bass. The jigging spoon is perfect when you're handling fish that are inactive because of water temperature levels that are too hot or too cold.

Tip # 15: Utilizing Dry Flies in the Afternoon

If you're fly fishing in the afternoon, you'll wish to utilize dry flies. The primary reason for this is that the sun is going to be warming the water and the air. And this indicates that you'll see hatches of little black flies. This is a good time to do some dry fly fishing because you can present a fly that resembles an adult bug.

Tip # 16: Keeping Track of Patterns

Keeping track of patterns: Something that you can do if you discover that your preferred fishing location is providing you trouble is to keep a log each time that you fish. Make note of the issues that you're having along with:

- weather conditions

- water temperature level

- current

- the size of the fish that you do capture

- the time of day that you fish

After a time period, you might see a pattern taking place, such as the absence of bites on days when the water temperature level is too hot or too cold. This will be your indicating element of what modifications you need to make to break your unfortunate streak, such as altering the time of day during which you fish or altering the side of the lake that you fish from.

Tip # 17: Basic Tools for Tying Flies

There are some fundamental tools that you'll require for tying flies. This involves:

- A bobbin to hold the thread while you're connecting.

- A vice to hold the hook while you're tying.

- Hackle pliers to maintain a firm hold on fragile and little plumes.

- Needlepoint scissors for trimming and cutting materials.

- A bodkin and half-hitch tool for assistance with tying the half-hitch knot.

- A vise material clip for holding all the materials strongly in one location.

- Head cement that is utilized for both gluing and to include a finish.

Tip # 18: Tying your Fly to the Tippet

You might discover that there are times when you have trouble tying the fly to the tippet. This can take place whether you remain in the water or up on the bank. An excellent technique to assist you is to hold the fly up against a background that is single-colored, like the sky. The background will have the ability to assist you in seeing the fly that much easier.

Tip # 19: Utilizing a Sub-Surface Fly

There is a technique to utilizing a sub-surface fly so that it captures more fish: deodorize the fly before you utilize it by scrubing it with mud or underwater plants. This is going to mask the chemical and human smells that are connected to it, which might sidetrack the fish from striking.

Tip # 20: Rods and Guides

Another element of your rod that you ought to learn more about is the guide, or the eyes. The guide is what sends the signals of the line to the rod so that it's simple for you to feel the fish on the other end. There are numerous various kinds of guides out there today.

Some guides have rings that are made from ceramic put inside the external metal frame. Still, other guides have inner rings that are made from silicone carbide, aluminum oxide, chrome plating, or gold aluminum oxide. The rings of the rod are what helps in the decrease of friction that can induce your line to fray.

The length of the rod handle is crucial along with what the rod is made from, such as foam or cork. You'll wish to select a rod handle that is still simple for you to hold if your hands end up being damp.

You will not wish to utilize a light action rod to capture fish given that you'll require a strong blank to be able to pull the fish out of its cover. A medium or medium/heavy rod is going to provide you with the strength that you require to take out the fish while at the same time offering you the versatility to utilize topwater baits. You may wish to utilize a trigger handle if you're utilizing a long-handled rod so that you have the manageability that you require.

Before you go out fishing ensure that you examine the guides on your rod. You wish to make sure that none of the guides are bent. Bent guides stop the line from moving through them properly. Clean out the inside of the circle of the guides before you begin fishing to guarantee that your line does not fray and break when you're drawing in the fish.

One last thing that you need to concentrate on when you're purchasing a brand-new rod is how the guides are connected to the rod. The wrapping needs to suffice so that the guides do not end up being loose.

Tip # 21: More Tips from the Professionals

The more tips and techniques that you have, the greater luck you'll take to your fly fishing. As a newbie, you'll wish to attempt a range of methods up until you discover what works best for you and the water that you're fishing in.

- Thick weeds: When you're fishing in thick weeds the most effective lure that you can utilize is a spinnerbait or a crankbait that is shallow running. Make certain that you cast parallel to the edge of the weed flow if you can. Keep in mind to look in the interior edges of weedbeds.

- Timber pileups: When you're fishing in deep timber, your primary focus is going to be not to get your line tangled up. Utilize a plastic worm or a jigging spoon for the greatest outcomes.

- Fishing from fallen trees: If you wish to fish from a fallen tree, make certain that you draw back your bait so that it runs in parallel to the tree limbs. This is since the water is extremely shallow and you do not wish to disrupt the location any more than you need to.

- Working the area: Ensure that you work the area that you're fishing in as extensively as possible. Try a couple of various lures if the very first one does not bring you success. You may wish to consider returning once again at a different time of day.

- Keep a close eye on your lines: Make certain that you keep an eye on your lines especially when you're recovering them. Keep in mind that when the weather condition is cold, the bass can strike and entirely miss the lures.

- Avoid excess noise: The more noise that you make, the less the bass is going to bite.

- Night fishing: Night fishing is an excellent choice in the summertime when the water temperature level throughout the day is simply too hot for bass to swim high in the water.

- Creeks and coves: Throughout the fall months, ensure that you have a look at creeks and coves because this is where baitfish tend to hover. This implies the bass will not be far behind.

- Utilizing surface plugs: When you're utilizing surface plugs, attempt to pay as much attention as you can to the angle of your rod. You ought to be holding the rod low when you have the lure near you and higher when the lure is further away.

Tips # 22: Leaders

When it pertains to leaders you have two options: you can purchase them or you can tie your own. In case you're going to tie your own, you'll wish to get a guidebook that demonstrates to you how to do this. If you're going to purchase them, you'll wish to search for a leader that is appropriate for the location where you are going to be fishing. For instance, if you're going fishing for bream (saltwater fly fishing), you'll wish to utilize a light leader that weighs about 2lbs.

Tip # 23: Knotless Tapered Leads

For freshwater fishing, it's ideal to utilize a knotless tapered lead instead of a knotted tapered lead. This is due to the fact that you will experience less tangles when you're casting and the leader will not get caught on debris that could be discovered in the water or on any free-standing structures.

Tip # 24: Learn to Read the Water

Fish will act in a different way depending upon specific water conditions that alter depending upon what season it is. This consists of the temperature level of the water, what the weather condition is like, and the volume of the water. If you wish to end up being an effective fly fisher, you'll need to find out how to read the waters where you're fishing.

A few of the things that you'll find as you learn to read the water are (1) throughout non-feeding periods, fish can still be motivated to strike if they remain in a deep pocket of water, and (2) when fish are feeding they are generally discovered in the shoreline of runs of pools and in mild water pockets.

Water chemistry plays a huge role in the health of fish, the area where they are discovered, and how effective you are at capturing the huge one. Among the most crucial elements of water chemistry is pH. In scientific terms, pH can be specified as the negative log molar concentration of hydronium ions in the water. In easy language, pH is the measure of the acidity or basicity in the water.

pH is normally assessed on a scale of 1 to 14. A pH of 7 is considered to be neutral. pH totals of less than 7 are acidic, while a measure of over 7 is considered basic.

A lot of fish have the ability to endure a vast array of pH in the waters where they live. This is since they have the capability to manage their internal levels of pH. This is achieved by the fish continuously changing the ratio of bases and acids within their systems. They make these modifications by expelling any excess acids in the urine and likewise by managing their breathing.

The quicker a fish breathes, the quicker the CO_2 leaves the blood, hence raising the level of pH in the blood. Nevertheless, the majority of fish are ultimately weakened by this continuous regulating of their system. If the fish lives for too long in an environment that is too acidic or too basic, it will end up being incapable of handling its own system chemistry. When this takes place the fish will stop feeding and ultimately pass away.

Tip # 25: Watch Out for Structures

When you're looking around for a location to cast your line, it is essential that you look around for structures both on and in the water. This can be a big stone, a log that is immersed, or the tail end of a pool. These are fantastic locations to discover fish because they do not wish to work really hard when it pertains to trying to find a meal. Fish will gather together near structures, where they will establish feeding stations.

Tip # 26: Fishing in the Early Season-- Night Fishing

As soon as the ice melts off of rivers and inland lakes, you can wager that it's time for fly fishing. Try to find dark-colored bays where the temperature level of the water will increase faster. You'll discover lots of bass and panfish in these waters. Early season fishing is a fantastic manner in which you can begin your fly fishing as early in the year as possible.

Night fishing for fish is generally practiced in those locations of the United States, where the weather is too hot and unpleasant to fish throughout the day. This consists of locations such as reservoirs in the southeast and west. When the weather condition is hot, numerous fish tend to go to deeper depths throughout the day and they can just be captured by night fishing. Throughout the night, when it's chillier, fish will go up to the shallower waters where they will eat crawfish.

Night fishing can be a great deal of fun; however, you want to take special preventative measures, such as knowing the location that you're fishing in and keeping in mind to use your life vest.

You'll understand when it's time to begin night fishing when the bigger fish stop biting throughout the hot day. Night fishing is typically practiced when there are water temperature levels that are in the middle '60s and warmer.

When it pertains to night fishing, there are 4 phases of the moon that you'll wish to take note of. The very best times to fish during the night will take place one time a month: 3 days before a complete or new moon and 3 days after a complete or new moon. This involves the day of the complete or new moon.

Tip # 27: Standard Casting

Standard casting is really straightforward: the fly line and the rod are both raised in a smooth motion. You'll utilize an up and backward direction in which you stop when the rod is exactly at the vertical point. When the line begins to straighten or fall downwards, the cast is going to start increasing in speed at the same time when your wrist snaps the whole rod back from the 11:00 and 1:00 clock positions. The line is going to they fly forward to where you wish it to land.

When you're prepared to cast, make it a long cast that moves right out from where you are standing. Pursue a ten-foot cast. When the bait strikes the bottom, wait for a minute or more before you begin to drag it gradually up along the slope. When you're prepared to cast once again, toss your line out a bit to the right. Then cast to the left the following time, so that you're fanning the location before you.

You likewise have the possibility of wading knee-deep out into the water to cast your line to ensure that it runs parallel to the bank. This enables you to fish the whole area of the bank to ensure that you have the most success.

Use clothing that is going to let you blend into the bank, like camouflage. And walk gently and meticulously as you stroll along the bank to avoid scaring the bass or other fish in the location. Make sure to move slowly at all times.

Fishing for fish from the bank can actually challenge you as a fly fisher. As soon as you get those initial couple of bites, you'll see that bank fishing is just as great as fishing in the stream or lake.

Tip # 28: Fishing in Stormy Weather

Fly fishing in stormy weather can come with its own specific obstacles. A storm happens when winds come up unexpectedly, without warning, and with no sign of how long the storm is going to last. One huge worry throughout a storm is a thunderstorm.

If you're out fishing and a storm happens, there are some preventative measures that you'll wish to take. You'll wish to head for greater ground instantly if you're near the water and there are thunderstorms in the location. If there is no indication of thunder or lightning, you might select to ride out the storm and continue fishing. In this case, you'll need to change your fishing method to mirror the adjustment in the weather condition.

When you're fishing along the coast and a storm appears, you can benefit from the wind. You'll typically have the ability to capture fish at really shallow levels in windy weather. Nevertheless, these will most likely be little bass. You'll discover larger fish at deeper depths throughout storms; however, these fish will be more difficult to capture and you must focus your efforts on the tinier ones.

Tip # 29: Etiquette and Rules you Want to Know

There are particular styles of etiquette and rules that you ought to follow when you're fishing for any kind of fish.

- "Do unto others as you would have them do unto you": Whenever you're fishing, whether on the coastline or in a boat, make certain that you deal with others the same way you would wish to be treated.

- Keep your distance: When you're fishing around other anglers, make certain that you keep a great distance far from them so that they have ample space. Take note of the direction that others are casting and provide them enough berth both in a boat and on the coastline.

- Keeping secrets: If somebody shares their preferred fishing location with you and asks that you do not give this area to others, you must honor the request.

- Get permission: If you wish to fish on personal property, such as a farm pond, make certain that you get permission initially. When you leave the location after fishing, it ought to look the same as when you showed up.

- Other fishers: Remember that not all fishers are bass fishers and that everybody deserves your regard regardless of what kind of fish they are fishing for.

- Fishing license: Depending upon where you live, there will various guidelines and policies for licensing. In a lot of states or provinces, you'll require a freshwater license if you wish to catch freshwater fish. Your fishing license must specify the kind of fish that you're going to be capturing. Constantly ensure that you understand the guidelines and policies of the lake, river, stream, or other water location that you're going to be fishing in. This involves when you can fish, where you can fish, and the number of fish you can take out of the water.

Tip # 30: Roll Casting

Roll casting is when your fly line is drawn back along the water throughout a back cast instead of being raised from the water. Throughout the forward cast, your line will likewise be drawn back along the water instead of being lifted. You'll wish to utilize a roll cast when you desire a little bit of leverage with back casting in locations where you do not have much space or if there is a strong wind that is drawing back on the line.

Tip # 31: Reach Casting

Throughout a reach cast the fly, leader, and line are presented to your target location at a broad angle from the left or right side of the caster. This enables you a lot of reach. Reach casting is really helpful when you wish to send a fly throughout a river or stream that has more than one speed of the current. The reach cast allows you to prevent your fly from being dragged downstream at a rate that is quicker than the water where it is expected to land.

Tip # 32: Slack Line Casting

Slack line casting is when the fly line has the ability to fall onto the water in what are called "s" curves. This kind of cast is going to let your fly float on the water with no dragging movement. You'll wish to utilize this cast when you're casting over a current or into a downstream.

Tip # 33: Shooting Line Casting

You'll wish to utilize this kind of cast when you wish to produce a cast that extends out more line. To achieve the shooting line cast, for either the forward or the backward cast, you want to utilize more power than you did when you cast the line as far as you did the initial time.

Tip # 34: Depend on Your Vision When Casting

There are going to be times when you want to rely on your vision in order to figure out the target that you are casting towards. This is especially true in tailwaters and spring creeks, where you'll want to stalk the fish before you cast for it. Utilize your eyes to determine your casting targets in particular ways like:

- Noting the shadow of a fish.

- Noting the riseform of a big fish.

- Noting the flash of a fish that is nymphing.

When you can determine the fish and its lie, you'll have the ability to properly place your target and prepare for the ideal cast.

Tip # 35: Utilizing a Hauling Method

The hauling method is when you increase the speed of your line by utilizing the strength of your rod arm and your free hand arm. To attain an excellent haul, you want to pull down on the fly line at the position simply beneath the stripper guide on your rod. The pull is going to increase the speed of the line as it moves outward. As you end up being more skilled, you can attempt a double haul, which is when you pull both the backward and the forward stroke with power.

Tip # 36: The Method of "Mending the Line"

The method of mending the line is when you rearrange your fly line and leader on top of the moving water. To achieve this method, all you want to do is utilize a range of motions such as roll-casting and raising the rod. When you're fishing in streams, you'll need to know how to mend your line so that you keep it straight and untangled.

Tip # 37: Match the Length of Your Tippet to the Hole

Among the most essential things that you can do when it pertains to effective fly fishing is matching the length of your tippet to the depth where the fish are and to the depth of the hole. From time to time, enable the weight to touch the bottom, ensuring that it does not drag. For example, if you have a tippet that is 6 feet long, it will put your fly about 2 to 4 feet off of the bottom.

Tip # 38: Utilizing a Slow-Action Rod

A slow-action rod is, in some cases, referred to as a full flex rod. This is among the simplest kinds of rod to cast, nevertheless, it can frequently be a bit too shaky for novices to utilize. This kind of rod isn't really reliable if you're fly fishing for bigger fish due to the fact that you will not have the ability to utilize the rod's butt tightness to hold up versus a strong fish. The slow-action rod is among the least costly rods that you can purchase.

Tip # 39: Fishing Etiquette-- The Right of Way

When it pertains to fishing rules, the right of way is something that you'll want to understand. The guideline is that the angler who is currently in the water is provided the right of way. The rule likewise applies if you're strolling along the bank or floating. If you want to move locations, attempt to move upriver whenever possible. You never ever wish to intrude on another fly fisher without asking initially. If you do get approval to go into the very same waters, make certain that you do so upriver and enable the other angler a great deal of room.

Tip # 40: Fishing Etiquette-- Taking out Your Line

Common courtesy says that you take your line out of the water for any angler who has a fish on the line. This is so that they have lots of area in order to land their fish. This rule is essential if you're fishing down-river from the other angler. Make certain that you never ever enter the area of an angler who is releasing or landing a fish on the bank.

Tip # 41: Fishing Etiquette – Silence

Whenever you're fly fishing, you'll want to be as silent as you can, and this suggests leaving your pet and the radio at home. There are 2 reasons why you wish to be as silent as possible: (1) you do not wish to startle the fish, and (2) you do not wish to disrupt other fly fishers. Lots of people delight in fly fishing for the peace and solitude that it provides them.

Tip # 42: Fishing Etiquette-- Provide a Helping Hand

Constantly be willing to assist other anglers. This can be as easy as helping them recover something that has actually floated down-river or lending them something that they require, such as an additional line. You're all there for an enjoyable day of fly fishing, so assisting each other out simply lends to the experience.

Tip # 43: Wading with Safety

When you're wading ensure that you follow a couple of standard guidelines: (1) never ever fish on your own on remote lakes, rivers, or streams, (2) use an excellent set of wading boots, (3) utilize a great wading staff that is versatile yet strong, and (4) understand the location where you're wading. Wading is a terrific method to get access to those locations that you could not otherwise reach.

Tip # 44: Tackle Boxes

Tackle boxes: A tackle box is a requirement so that you can keep all your "things" with you in one arranged location. A few of the things to bear in mind when you utilize a tackle box and wish to stay away from overfilling include:

- Keep your worms and soft plastic bait in a little container far from your other lures. This is going to keep the soft plastic lures from producing a chemical reaction with the components that other baits are constructed from.

- Purchase 2 or more little tackle boxes to hold particular groups of lures. For example, purchase one tackle box to hold your worms and another to hold your spinnerbaits.

- Purchase seasonal tackle boxes that you just utilize at specific times of the year. In the spring, you can have a tackle box which contains jigs, plastic worms, and minnow lures. And in the fall, you can have a tackle box that is loaded with fall lures, like topwaters and crankbaits.

Tip # 45: Keep your Fishing Vest Organized

If you utilize a fishing vest to carry around your tackle and lure, you'll wish to keep it as arranged as you can so that you're not fumbling around trying to find something when you require it. If you're not going to be utilizing something, leave it home so that you just bring the must-haves.

Tip # 46: Carry a Wading Staff

When you're fishing in water that is rough or unknown, you may wish to bring a wading staff to keep you steady and provide you with much better footing.

Tip # 47: Wear Great Shoes

A great set of wading shoes will let your grip the bottom that you're walking on. Select shoes that have soles with rubber cleats because these are perfect for bottoms that are full of mud, fine gravel, sand, or soft silt.

Tip # 48: Bring the Sun Block

Although it might appear like a little tip to point out, bringing the sunblock is something that you do not wish to forget. After standing in a sunny stream for 8 hours, you'll be pleased that you remembered to bring along some protection.

Tip # 49: Utilize Polarized Glasses

Using polarized glasses is among the very best things that you can do. You'll have the ability to see below the water so you can keep an eye on your fish. Do not forget a hat to minimize the quantity of glare that you experience.

Tip # 50: Discouraging Insects

If you wish to dissuade pests, you'll wish to stay away from wearing clothing that is red, yellow, black, white, or navy blue. These colors can bring in black flies, deerflies, gnats, and mosquitoes.

Tip # 51: Dress for the Weather condition

Use the appropriate kind of clothing for the weather condition. You do not wish to be stuck in a rainstorm without protective equipment. Bear in mind that it's constantly easier to remove a layer of clothes than it is to be without anything to put on.

Tip # 52: Sticking to the Fundamentals

Attempt to stay with the fundamentals whenever possible. This implies bringing a couple of little boxes of flies with you and fishing them to death. Numerous professionals utilize just a floating line for the majority of the fish that they capture and they make a point of keeping their tackle to a minimum. Lots of beginner fly fishers fall under the trap of using a lot of "brand-new patterns." Stick to a pattern and fish it for around 3 to 4 dozen drifts. This will bring you the greatest outcomes.

Tip # 53: What is Vital Equipment?

When it pertains to fly fishing, there is equipment that is vital and equipment that is less vital. Concentrate on bringing the necessary equipment that focuses on the day of fishing ahead. Listed below is the necessary equipment:

- An excellent rod that you can count on.

- A reel.

- A range of bait that you will be utilizing that day.

- A range of flies and lures that you will be utilizing that day.

- A first aid kit.

- A rain jacket.

- A hat and sunblock.

- Additional clothes that you can use and remove if it gets too hot.

Listed below is non-essential equipment:

- A big tackle box that is stuffed with all your lures, baits, and flies.

- Things that you will not be utilizing on that fishing day, such as the incorrect line or reel.

Tip # 54: The Size of your Flies

The size of your flies will matter, particularly in the spring and fall when there are high waters, at which time you'll need bigger flies than you would be utilizing in the summertime. Summertime brings lower water levels and you can get away with utilizing smaller sized flies. Throughout those months when you're not fly fishing, put in the time to bind various sizes of flies and develop your selection. This will conserve you time when you are fishing.

Tip # 55: Fly Fishing for Salmon-- Mood Matters

Salmon can be an odd fish to capture considering that their state of mind frequently matters. If they remain in a "taking" state of mind, they will accept any lure and bait. Nevertheless, if they are not in a taking state of mind, they will neglect anything that you hang in front of them.

Tip # 56: Fly Fishing for Salmon-- When Will they Strike?

When salmon remain in the river, they will not be feeding. Nevertheless, this does not imply that they will not be striking. For salmon, striking is a natural behavior. While the salmon lie in a lake, they will be rather predatory and loaded with hostility. They will continue this behavior when they go into the river. This benefits you since you get those strikes, whether they are feeding or not.

Tip # 57: Fly Fishing for Salmon-- Keep your Hooks Sharp

The salmon has an extremely thick jaw, so you'll wish to keep your hooks as sharp as possible so that they can permeate deep.

Tip # 58: Fly Fishing for Salmon-- Fishing with a Partner

Attempt fly fishing for salmon with a partner to ensure that you can identify more fish. Take turns fly fishing. One partner will fish while the other one stands on the opposite bank and watches the behavior of the salmon and precisely where they are. Ensure that you bring along your polarized glasses.

Tip # 59: Fly Fishing for Salmon-- Locate an Excellent Hole

Make an effort to discover a hole that has a lot of salmon in it. These kinds of holes can be fished throughout the day.

Tip # 60: Fly Fishing for Salmon-- Select Low-Light Days-- Cool Water

Salmon like days that have a low-light or cloud cover. On days that are bright, you'll most likely discover salmon gathering together far from the brightness in deep holes. It's those cloudy days that will make the salmon more available to you.

Water temperature level, and understanding what it is, can play a huge part in the success or failure of salmon fishing. You'll wish to purchase an excellent thermometer so that you can monitor water temperature levels throughout the day. Make certain that you position the thermometer in the exact same location each time at a depth of anywhere from 6 inches to 3 feet beneath the surface.

Keep a note pad with a record of water temperature levels, making sure to update whenever you can. After a couple of years of recording the water temperature level in your preferred fishing area, you'll have an excellent idea of which patterns are taking place.

Salmon do far better in cooler water. When water temperature levels begin to increase, salmon go deeper. This is due to the fact that there is more oxygen in cooler water and salmon require this oxygen to endure. Salmon will be more active in cooler water than warm water, so they will be a bit harder to capture as they fight harder to leave. You'll wish to discover a middle ground in the water temperature level so that the fish aren't too active.

Comprehending the water temperature level of the water that you are fishing in can play a huge part in understanding what kind of rod, reel, and line to utilize along with what kind of lures and baits you must be utilizing.

Tip # 61: Fly Fishing for Salmon-- Where to Fish and When to Fish

Salmon like to collect in dark and deep pools where the water is dark and black. You'll likewise discover them on the cusp of bends at the point where the water begins to get deep. This fish likes water to be quick on the top and sluggish lower down. The salmon's behavior throughout the day will trigger it to swim up or down depending upon the brightness of the day and the temperature level of the water.

There are no right and wrong guidelines about when to fish for salmon. If you just have time to fish on weekends, you'll need to take the weather condition as it is. This suggests learning to adjust to all kinds of weather conditions. For example, when the weather condition is especially windy, you'll need to understand which line and reel are best so that you can cast far. You'll likewise need to discover how to cast into the wind so that your line casts out far enough. Among the most essential things that you want to think about when it's windy is your security. What you typically see on a calm day, such as logs and brush, can be concealed by the waves that the wind generates.

As weather conditions alter, you'll need to learn to alter with them or you might never ever capture those salmon that you have actually been dying to take home.

Tip # 62: Fly Fishing for Salmon-- Discovering the Snags

Considering that salmon like to gather in deep holes, you can expect there to be snags that are going to grab on to your flies. Before you find yourself losing a lot of flies, take a while to access the hole before you begin fishing. Discover a high spot, if you can, and utilize your polarized glasses to look down into the hole to see if you can find any snags. Another technique is to utilize a fly that you do not mind losing and send it into the hole to see what occurs.

Tip # 63: Fly Fishing for Salmon-- Examine the Tail End of Pools

Make certain that you inspect the tail end of pools in addition to the neck location. Salmon like to gather in this area so you'll generally discover more than an abundance of fish.

Tip # 64: Fly Fishing for Salmon-- Learn to Fish Gradually

Among the huge errors that beginner fly fishers make is to fish for salmon too rapidly. Although helpful for trout fishing, salmon need to be fished with more perseverance.

Tip # 65: Fly Fishing for Trout - Utilizing a Shorter Rod

When you're fishing for trout, you need to be utilizing a rod that is rather short, like an 8ft brook rod or a 10ft loch job. You wish to ensure that your rod fits the location that you're fishing in. The one thing that you want to remember is that a brief rod is hard to use if you wish to get any range.

Tip # 66: Fly Fishing for Trout-- Utilizing a Floating Line

There are numerous trout fly lines that you can select from when you're fishing for this kind of fish. Newbie fly fishers must start with a floating line, given that it will be a lot easier for them to control.

Tip # 67: Fly Fishing for Trout-- Dry Fly or Wet Fly?

Understanding what fly to utilize is rather basic when it pertains to fishing for trout: utilize a dry fly if the trout are feeding upon the surface and utilize a damp fly if they are feeding beneath the surface.

Tip # 68: Fly Fishing for Trout - When to Change your Fly

If you discover that the trout aren't biting continue to utilize the exact same fly for about 15 minutes before you change to another one. Maintain this pattern up until you discover a fly that works.

Tip # 69: Fly Fishing for Trout-- Trout Behaviors

Trout are simple to anticipate. Rainbow trout constantly swim in shoals while the brown trout are more territorial and stay away from this pattern. The one huge thing to bear in mind when you're fly fishing for trout is that you typically want to go to them instead of expecting them to come to you.

A fast note on trout habits in lakes: Lakes in higher locations are typically much rockier than lower-lying lakes. These kinds of lakes will not have a good deal of weed or brush cover. You'll discover rocky lakes a bit hard to fish in considering that the water is too clear and there aren't a lot of locations where trout can discover the cover. If there are any trout in the lake, they will probably be of the large size given that they take pleasure in deeper waters and clear conditions.

Numerous knowledgeable fly fishers take pleasure in fishing from the bank of a lake even if they own a boat. Among the first things that you want to do is to discover the ideal bank. Try to find banks that have about a thirty-degree slope that runs away from the shoreline. The water in the location ought to be anywhere from 5 to 15 feet deep. If the slope if more than forty-five degrees you'll have difficulty balancing and remaining in a fixed position.

Trout are drawn in to really steady slopes and will typically accumulate in this kind of environment. If there is a little bit of greenery or brush that has actually been immersed, the trout will enjoy the location a lot more.

When you're fishing from the bank, you'll wish to utilize spinning tackle. Put the weight about 8 to twelve inches far from the hook. The very best kinds of lures to utilize are spinnerbaits and crankbaits. Stay away from utilizing a jig due to the fact that you'll discover that it gets up much too often. To spare yourself the trouble of bringing a tackle box, consider wearing a vest where you can keep all your tackle in practical pockets.

Tip # 70: Fly Fishing for Trout-- Releasing your Trout

There are going to be some trophies that you wish to photograph; however, a lot of times, you'll wish to make certain that you do not handle the trout. Trout are covered in a protective layer of slime and when you touch it, you disrupt the great balance of things. Trout can establish fungi on the locations where you touch, which can destroy it. To release the trout, all you want to do is to release the hook from the mouth and enable it to swim away without touching it. For assistance in getting rid of the hook, you can utilize forceps or little pliers.

Tip # 71: Fly Fishing for Trout-- Revive prior to Releasing

Before you release the trout, you want to ensure that it is totally revived ahead of time. If the fish is actually tired, it might turn over upside down or roll onto its side. Bigger trout will take more time to revive while little fish generally need no reviving at all.

If you want to revive a fish, ensure that you hold it so that it is upright. Look for a flow of water that is rather mild, simply enough so that you can get its gills working and so that it can get oxygen back from the water. As the fish begins to revive, its gills are going to begin to work more and more up until it can remain upright in the water. The objective is to enable the trout to swim away without your assistance.

Tip # 72: Fly Fishing for Trout-- The Significance of Reading the Stream

When you have the ability to read the river or stream, you increase your odds of capturing that trout. Many streams will have a current that produces a pattern that is referred to as the riffle-run-pool pattern. This pattern is going to continue to duplicate itself over and over again. You'll discover huge brown trouts in deep pools while the tinier brown and rainbow trout can be discovered in runs. The riffles will include little trout throughout day hours and larger trout throughout the morning and evening feeding times.

Lots of fly fishers neglect streams in favor of lakes or rivers. This, nevertheless, can be a huge error. Streams offer excellent options for fly fishing, particularly those streams that have cool water. Trout appear to take pleasure in streams, given that they can live in deep holes that are discovered simply beneath the rapids. They likewise delight in hovering underneath undercut banks, given that the water current here is calmer yet still has a flow to it.

Tip # 73: Fly Fishing for Trout - Identifying the Riffle

Riffles will have a current that is quick, in addition to really shallow water. The bottom is going to be a mix of debris, gravel, or stones. You'll wish to fish riffles throughout the morning or the evening throughout feeding durations.

Tip # 74: Fly Fishing for Trout-- Recognizing the Runs

Runs are much deeper than riffles; however, they have a more moderate current. You'll usually discover runs in between the riffles and the pools.

The bottom of runs is made up of debris or little gravel. Runs are terrific locations to discover trout at nearly any time.

Tip # 75: Fly Fishing for Trout-- Recognizing Pools

Pools are going to be darker than other locations of the river or stream. They have a much smoother current. The water is going to be slow-moving and deep over a bottom that is made up of sand, little gravel, or silt. You'll discover medium to big trout in pools throughout the midday.

Fishing for fish in natural lakes could be all the way from good to exceptional. The success that you have will typically depend upon what part of the nation the lake is located in. For example, the southern states have natural lakes that are rather shallow.

Lots of smaller sized natural lakes have a circular shape. You'll wish to focus your fishing technique near the coast where there are weeds and rocks. Bigger lakes, particularly, those lakes in the north, will typically have fantastic locations for trout to school. This can consist of islands, weed flows, natural reefs, and deep holes. Something to remember when it pertains to northern natural lakes is that they are typically sterile. This implies that although the water is extremely clear, it does not consist of big quantities of algae or plankton, and hence does not have a good deal of oxygen.

Tip # 76: Fly Fishing for Trout-- The Smart Fish

There are brand-new studies out that reveal that trout can quickly learn to navigate a labyrinth, and that they can recall the pattern for about 9 months. This suggests that in streams that are intensely fished, trout rapidly find out that motion on particular paths of pools is an indicator that there is a threat. The trout will frighten more quickly, considering that they understand the pattern of approaching fly fishers. What does this mean for you? Avoid approaching the very same pools in the same direction. Rather, discover various angles of approaches whenever you fish in that location.

Tip # 77: Fly Fishing for Trout-- Cool Water Fish

Trout like the cooler waters. When the water temperature level begins to increase in the summertime, the trout will relocate to much deeper and cooler waters. Not just will the water be cooler and deeper, there will be more oxygen in the water. When trout remain in water that is too warm and is lacking in oxygen, they begin to end up being upset.

By late summertime, trout will relocate to fast-moving riffles even if the water is hardly deep enough to cover them. You'll need to approach them meticulously. Let your fly drift to the tiniest spot of the riffle. Ensure that you cover the whole riffle before you carry on to the next area.

One essential thing to bear in mind is that the senses of feeling and hearing in a fish are practically identical. Trout feel and hear the vibration of motion and noise in the water. Each noise will have a different kind of pitch that sends out vibrations through the water. Trout have the ability to end up being acquainted with specific noises and pitches so that they have the ability to discover even the tiniest motion in the water. The feeling and hearing senses in a trout act practically as an integrated radar.

Just as with feeling and hearing, the way a trout smells and tastes is linked together as one sense. Many fish have taste buds on the interior and exterior of their mouths. This suggests that they have the ability to taste something before they have it in their mouth. This is why the bait that you utilize needs to be pleasing to the trout or it will not enter its mouth. And if it does enter into the fish's mouth, it will be rapidly spit out if it is undesirable.

Tip # 78: Fly Fishing for Trout - Recognizing Rises

Before you pick your fly you want to determine the feeding patterns of the trout:

- Sip Rise: A sip rise will have surface rings that are, in some cases, extremely difficult to see and ,in other times, extremely simple to see. A sip rise is brought on by a trout that is sucking used spinner or sipping on small duns.

- Dorsal Fin and Tail Rise: This rise is a sign that the trout are feeding just beneath the surface and that they will most likely overlook any surface flies.

- Head Rise: A head rise is identified by trout sticking their heads up out of the water. This suggests that they are eating mayfly, stonefly grownups, caddis grownups, or cripples and that they are going to feed right on the surface.

- Splashy Surge: A splashy surge shows that the trout will probably chase any whitebait or smelt into shallow waters.

A quick note on rivers: Rivers are most likely the ideal kind of environment for trout. This is due to the fact that they have a lot of oxygen in the water that is uniformly dispersed from top to bottom. The water temperature in rivers is a bit milder than lake temperatures.

When you're fishing for trout in rivers, you'll wish to remain near to the current but out of the direct flow. Search for breaks in the current such as stumps or logs; these are typically the locations where you'll discover trout hovering in schools.

River bars are likewise excellent locations to fish for trout. Do not neglect river bends as other great alternatives considering that trout appear to take pleasure in these serene locations.

Tip # 79: Fly Fishing for Trout-- Undercut Banks

Undercut banks are an excellent place to discover trout because this place offers them with outstanding cover from predators. The trout can hover against the edge of the stream right where the friction induces the water to decelerate, making the swimming simple.

A Woolly Bugger is perfect in this circumstance. You'll wish to cast upstream so that your fly and your leader can land near to the bank and nearly parallel to it. You can cast throughout the stream to fish if the stream is large enough. In this manner, your cast will land the fly near the undercut bank. When this occurs, you want to jig your cast downstream to ensure that as much of your fly line and the leader is lying in a parallel position to the bank as possible.

When the fly begins to drift downstream and gets drawn in by the current, you'll wish to flick the tip of your rod and press the fly line even more downstream. This action ought to bring in the attention of the most evasive trout.

Tip # 80: Utilizing a List

Utilizing a list can be among the very best things that you can do as you begin discovering the ins and outs of fly fishing. There are numerous things that you can place on your list involving (1) tracking your most effective fishing holes; (2) reminders to do things like honing your flies after a snag, (3) what lures work most effectively for you, (4) the most effective times to fish the river. Lists can keep you arranged and on track.

Tip # 81: Take a Fishing Trip

Take a fishing trip with a local guide. You'll find out a lot about how your guide watches the river or lake and what you need to do to attain that exact same knowledge. Take a trip close to home or travel abroad to experience worldwide fly fishing.

Tip # 82: Fishing in Dam-Controlled Waters

It's essential that when you're fishing in waters that are managed by a dam that you learn ahead of time when there will be a water release. The release will be signified by a horn or whistle, so make certain that you listen for the alert.

Tip # 83: Fishing Upstream

A fundamental principle of fly fishing is that a hooked fish isn't actually captured up until you have it up on the bank. If you wish to land more fish, the one thing that you may do is attempt to hook more fish upstream rather than downstream. By doing this, your fly will have a better chance of entering the jaw of the fish. Try to keep downstream of any fish that you have actually managed to hook; when the fish is downstream, it is utilizing less energy given that the current of the water is going to be doing much of the work for the fish.

Tip # 84: Sign Up With a Fly Fishing Club

Among the very best things that you can do as a novice fly fisher is to sign up with a fly fishing club. You'll get to know other anglers in the location where you live and might even have the ability to discover a fishing friend or more. The other advantage is that you can find out more about a few of the terrific angling places in your home area.

Tip # 85: Utilizing a Landing Net

If you wish to utilize a landing net, you want to make certain to hold the net on the stream bed and raise it up as the fish swims over top of it. A lot of fish are going to be lost after they make their last rush if they are confronted with a landing net that is being held vertically out in front of them. Besides, you can't expect the fish to wish to swim right into it! And in case you hold the web from behind and attempt to sweep up the fish, all are going to be lost. All it requires is one touch of the fish's tail and it will be gone.

Fish are known for their intense sense of vision. They have the ability to see in all kinds of water conditions and can see similarly well throughout the day and night. The reason for this terrific sight is that fish have eyes that have the ability to adjust naturally to various conditions of light. Regardless of what the color of the water is, they have the ability to count on their vision to direct them. At those times when the vision of the fish is limited, its other senses are going to kick in. This suggests that no matter where you hold that landing net, the fish will have the ability to see it or feel it.

Tip # 86: Storing your Rod

The one and only thing that you want to do to keep your rod in terrific shape is to store it properly. The first thing that you want to do is store the rod in the sock and a tough tube. In this manner, absolutely nothing can harm it when you're not utilizing it. After you're done utilizing your rod, ensure that you clean it. All of the salt must be rubbed off, and the rod left up until it is entirely dry before you put it away.

When you're cleaning your rod, utilize warm water that has actually been laced with moderate soap. Utilize a soft fabric. Ensure that you clean all parts of the rod, including the rod guides, feet, cork grip, and the reel. When you're done, make the effort to wash the rod with warm water. This procedure will keep your rod looking and executing excellent for a number of years.

Tip # 87: Keeping your Reels Covered

When you're not utilizing your reels, you must keep them covered. If you keep your reel exposed, you'll wind up with grit and dirt within it. Also, the external coating of your reel can be harmed and this can cause rust. If you wind up with scratches on the reel, you can cover the locations with clear fingernail polish to decelerate the corrosion.

Tip # 88: Avoid Windy Days

Newbie fly fishers might wish to avoid learning on windy days. Days that have any degree of wind will call for specific abilities for casting. As you're beginning learning how to fly fish, you'll wish to pick calm days so that you can practice your casting and other strategies.

Tip # 89: In Some Cases, it's Ideal to Do Absolutely Nothing

Fly fishing might appear like it's an active sport considering that you're constantly doing something, preparing something, and thinking of what you're going to be doing next. Nevertheless, often it's ideal to do absolutely nothing at all. Be patient, stand still, and simply take pleasure in the experience. The bottom line is that there are times when you need to wait to capture your fish.

Tip # 90: A Word about Nymphs

When you're fishing throughout the early spring months, the majority of the fish that you capture will be nymphs. The tough part about fishing for nymphs is picking the best pattern to utilize. Keep this tip in mind: fish with 2 flies since this doubles your odds of capturing one.

Tip # 91: Getting that Bonus Strike

Something that every fly fisher anticipates is that bonus strike. One manner in which you can get a bonus strike when you're at the completion of drift with a dry fly or nymph is to let your fly swing around. Then allow the fly to lie in the current for about 30 seconds to see if you get that bonus hit.

Tip # 92: Treating Fish Carefully

The majority of the fish that you capture when you're fly fishing will have delicate spots such as their mouths and gills. Manage them carefully when you eliminate the fly so that you do not harm them. And keep in mind that some fish have sharp teeth, so avoid putting your fingers inside the mouth.

Tip # 93: Fishing Near White Rocks

If you're searching for success, look for some white rocks to fish near. White rocks in a dark streambed can offer you with a lighter background. This will enable the fish to see a dark-colored bug or lure as it drifts over the contrasting colors of white rock and dark water. This can typically end in an excellent strike for you.

Tip # 94: Big Predator Fish and Low Light

When you blend a big predator fish with low light levels, you wind up with a fish that exercises less care and is more hostile than when the light is high. Fantastic days for fishing for big predators are at sunrise, at sundown, when there is stormy weather, and after the sun goes down.

Tip # 95: On your Way to Experience

As a newbie fly fisher, you'll wish to concentrate on ending up being more skilled. Following are a few of the leading tips for fly fishing from the professionals:

- Utilizing two lures on one line: If you're fishing in deep, clear water, you might wish to put 2 lures on one line. This is especially great if you wish to make a "vertical" presentation. You'll wish to utilize a bell sinker as the weight for included effect. Ensure that you tie 2 hooks onto the fishing line a couple of feet apart from one another.

- Utilizing a little spinner: There will be times when you wish to bring in fish by utilizing noise and sight. At these times, a little spinning blade is your best bet. Connect a little spinner to the end of a light weighted jig. This can be a really helpful method in cooler waters.

- Two-handed pitch cast: When you're fishing in close quarters, you may wish to attempt a two-handed pitch cast. Holding the lure in your left hand, pull on your rod so that you bring the tip down simply a bit. Offer the rod a little tip flex and after that swing up the tip at the same time that you release the lure. You ought to discover that the lure moves in a low motion towards your target location.

- Minnow-shaped plugs: Attempt fishing with a little minnow-shaped plug which will float above the bottom and is going to dart similar to a fish when you twitch the line.

Tip # 96: Fish and Noise

When you're fly fishing, you ought to remember that you'll be discovered more by the fish from "sound" than you will by sight. When you're walking or wading, make certain that you stroll gently and carefully. You'll wish to use shoes that have soles that do not make loud noises against bottom gravel and rocks.

Tip # 97: Understand the Language

The more you understand the language, or terminology, of fly fishing, the more enjoyable it will be as you fly fish with your family and friends. A few of the terms that you need to understand include:

- Fly: The fly is a light-weight lure that is utilized to draw in a range of fish consisting of trout and salmon. The most typical fly is the mayfly.

- Leader: The leader is connected to the end of the fly line because the fly line is too thick to hold flies. The leader can be identified as a tapered clear piece of monofilament.

- Plug: The plug is a lure that looks much like a bait fish. It will have several hooks that hang down from its body. You can utilize various plugs and jerk them around to appear like a fish that has actually been hurt.

- Spinners: A spinner is a little oval-shaped blade that is connected to the end of a lure. A spinning hook is going to be trailing off the end of it.

- Tippet: The tippet is a clear piece of monofilament. It is connected to the end of the leader so that the leader's end taper is maintained.

- Woolly Bugger: The Woolly Bugger is a fly that has a really easy design with a long tail plume on the end. This fly is well-known amongst knowledgeable fly fishers.

Tip # 98: Often the Fish are in Charge

There will be times when fish will take anything that you provide, no matter if it's similar to the bugs and foods that they are eating or how the bait acts. Then there will be other times when, regardless of what you provide, they will not strike at all. There is a popular quote that fits in well here:

" It is possible to deceive all of the fish a few of the time, and a few of the fish all of the time, it is nevertheless well nigh inconceivable to deceive all of the fish all of the time."

Tip # 99: Smoking your Fish

If you're going to be smoking your fish, it is necessary that you do not smoke it right after you have actually salted it. Let the fish sit overnight in a location that is cool and dry, enabling the surface to dry. This is going to seal in the flavors when the fish is smoked.

When you're ready to smoke the fish follow these instructions:

- Line the base of the smoker with foil, putting wood shavings atop the foil.

- Smoke the fish for approximately 8 hours for maximum flavor.

- When the smoking is done, cover the foil with the ashes and any of the juices that have actually dripped. This will leave your smoker tidy and prepared for the next usage.

Tip # 100: Fish ... Do Not Cast!

Do not simply spend your day casting. Novices frequently make the error of spending the entire day casting at every riffle, undercut bank, and other most likely looking for a fishing location without ever attaining success. And the end outcome is normally that the fly is taken away at that moment that they are taking a look at their fly box for their next cast. This is the moment to go back and think so that you can get a strike or two.

Take a while to think of what your fly is doing, what the fish are doing, what the weather is like, and what kind of fish you believe you may discover!

Fly fishing can be either excellent or really bad. Even when you have a fantastic technique in place, there are going to simply be times when the fish will not be biting. These are the days when you need to work even harder on your method so that you take home that reward.

There will be those days when you have actually prepared to fish in shallow water, yet the weather is simply too calm. You'll discover that in this circumstance, the very best time of day to fish is either throughout the low light of the morning or the low light of the day when it is more difficult for the bass to see you. Change your technique if you need to.

Another reason why the fish simply will not be biting is when the day is extremely bright and clear. These conditions create restrictions when it pertains to fly fishing, such as (1) the fish having the ability to see you, and (2) the water ending up being too hot, sending the fish to much deeper depths. With these conditions present, you'll need to be really sneaky in your pursuit of any fish. If you're going to making long casts, you will not need to fret excessively about stealth given that fish in deeper water will be less distracted by the intense light.

I hope that you enjoyed reading through this book and that you have found it useful. If you want to share your thoughts on this book, you can do so by leaving a review on the Amazon page. Have a great rest of the day.

Made in the USA
Middletown, DE
17 June 2020